GRAYWOLF PRESS

WARRIOR

— for —

GRINGOSTROIKA

ESSAYS, PERFORMANCE TEXTS, AND POETRY

BY

Guillermo Gómez-Peña

1605 — 1002

INTRODUCTION

BY

ROGER BARTRA

DOUGLAS KEILLER, ASSOCIATE EDITOR

Published by GRAYWOLF PRESS
2402 University Avenue, Suite 203
Saint Paul, Minnesota 55114
All rights reserved.

Printed in Canada

2 4 6 8 9 7 5 3
First Printing, 1993

Library of Congress Cataloging-in-Publication Data
Gómez-Peña, Guillermo
Warrior for gringostroika / by Guillermo Gómez-Peña ;
introduction by Roger Bartra
p. cm.
ISBN 1-55597-199-7 (pbk.)
1. Mexican Americans—Literary collections. 2. Mexican Americans—
Civilization. 3. Performance art—United States   I. Title
PS3557.O459W37   1993
814'.54—dc20   93-14529

Publication of this volume is made possible in part by a grant
provided by the Minnesota State Arts Board through an appropriation
by the Minnesota State Legislature, and by a grant from the
National Endowment for the Arts. Additional support has been
provided by the Andrew W. Mellon Foundation, the Lila Wallace-
Reader's Digest Fund, the McKnight Foundation, the
Dayton-Hudson Foundation for Dayton's and Target stores, the
Cowles Media Foundation, the General Mills Foundation,
and other generous contributions from foundations, corporations, and
individuals. Graywolf Press is a member agency of United Arts,
Saint Paul. To these organizations and individuals who make our work
possible, we offer heartfelt thanks.

ACKNOWLEDGMENTS

Many of the essays, performance pieces, and poems have been published previously in multiple formats in the spirit of the author's desire to provide wide access for his ideas.

"A Binational Performance Pilgrimage" has also appeared in *The Drama Review,* Fall 1991; in *Third Text,* London, Fall 1992; and in the catalogue of the exhibit, "Sin Frontera: Chicano Arts from the Border States of the U.S.," *Cornerhouse,* Manchester, 1993.

"Documented/Undocumented" was first published in *La Jornada Semanal* (Mexico City), October 25, 1987. An English version of this work as translated by Rubén Martinez was published in *L.A. Weekly,* and in *The Graywolf Annual Five: Multicultural Literacy,* Graywolf Press, 1988. It was also published in the catalogue of the French exhibit, "The Demons of Los Angeles," 1989.

"The Border Is..." previously appeared in *Pus Moderna* (Mexico City), 1991; and in *Museums and Communities: The Politics of Public Culture,* The Smithsonian Institution, 1992.

"The Multicultural Paradigm" was published in *High Performance,* Fall 1989; and in *La Jornada Semanal* (Mexico City), February 25, 1990. It also appeared under a different title in the exhibition catalogue of "Decade," co-curated by the New Museum, the Studio Museum of Harlem, and MOCHA (New York), 1990.

"From Art-mageddon to Gringostroika" was first published in *High Performance,* Fall 1991; and in the exhibition catalogue of "The Hybrid State" at Exit Art, New York, 1992. It appeared in the catalogue for the show, "Counter-Colonialismo," co-curated by MARS, Phoenix; Mexic-arte, Austin; and the Centro Cultural de la Raza, San Diego, 1992.

Califas was published in *The Broken Line/La Linea Quebrada,* March 1987, and in *The Politics of Everyday Fear,* edited by Brian Massumi, University of Minnesota Press, 1993. It was used as the narrative for Philip Brookman's film about Chicano art *Mi Otro Yo (My Other Self),* 1988, and an excerpt of the performance was filmed by Louis Malle for the documentary *And the Pursuit of Happiness,* 1987.

Border Brujo premiered at the Border Arts Workshop's "Border Realities IV: Casa de Cambio" project at the Centro Cultural de la Raza, San Diego, 1988. In January 1990 it became the film *Border Brujo,* directed by Isaac Artenstein, Lynn Schuette, Executive Producer, and distributed by Video Data Bank (Chicago), Third World Newsreel (New York), and Cinewest Productions (San Diego). Different versions of the script were published in *Being America,* White Pine Press, 1991; *The Drama Review,* Fall 1991; and in *Whitewalls,* No. 21, Winter 1989.

1992 is adapted from the *1992* trilogy. *1990* premiered in 1990 at the Temporary Contemporary Museum of Contemporary Art, Los Angeles, as part of the Los Angeles Film Festival. (A version for radio was produced by "Crossroads," Miami, with the title "1990: Border Notebooks.") *1991* premiered at the Brooklyn Academy of Music in 1991, as part of the Next Wave Festival. Different versions of the text have been published in *Whitewalls,* Nos. 30 and 31, Chicago, 1992, and in *Walks on Water,* Methuen Press, London, 1992. A documentary, *1992: The Rediscovery of America by the Warrior for Gringostroika,* was produced by WGBH, Boston, 1992.

"Open Letter" previously appeared in *Shift* magazine, a publication of Artspace, San Francisco, 1992.

• to my queridísima Coco, la Yemaya de Brooklyn, who has dared to love me as much as I love her

• to my adored son Guillermito, el mini-brujo, who has taught me to see the world as a gigantic poem once again

• to the memory of my father Guillermo who patiently waits for me on the other side of life

• to my mother Martha who hid me so many times under her skirt

• to grandma Pipa who was born with the century. Her eyes have seen it all. Abuela, will you be alive to read my book?

• to the memory of Ralph Madariaga, Luke Theodore Morrison, Eva García, Alfonso Metaca, and Carlos Gómez-Navarro, who decided to part a bit earlier

• to my conceptual godfather Felipe Ehrenberg

• to my Chicano godparents, Amalia Mesa-Bains and Tomas Ybarra Frausto

• to Marco Vinicio González, Isaac Artenstein, and Alfredo Araico, compañeros de mil cruces, tocadas y desmadres perfórmicos

• to Saint Nola Mariano, Holy Protector of my (wet)back in the dangerous U.S. art world

• to my maestros of interdisciplinary troublemaking, Linda Burnham, Steve Durland, René Yañez, Peter Sellars, Richard Scheckner, Shifra Goldman, Roger Bartra, Pedro Rodríguez, Rupert García, Juan Carrillo, Rasheed Araeen, and Cesar Espinoza

• to all the locos and locas who are always willing to cross the border with me without papers: my carnalísimos Robert Sánchez, Roberto Sifuentes, Rubén Martínez, Yareli Arismendi, Iñigo Manglano, Deedee Halleck, María Martin, Danny Salazar, Jessica Haggedorn, Gustavo Vázquez, Elia Arce, Oscar Garza, John Malpede, Tim Miller, Catherine Lord, Joe Lambert, Rubén Guevara, Ellen Sebastian, Enrique Chagoya, Suzanne Lacey, Anne Chamberlain, Beto Arcos, Richard Lou, Marco Anguiano, María Hinojosa, Keith Antar Mason, Deborah Levy, James Luna, Sergio "Quetzalcoke" Arau, Jude Eberhart, Encarnación Teruel, Kim Sawchuck, Hugo Sánchez, Jeanette Ingberman, Papo Colo, Denise Mayotte, Sal Salerno, Max Aguilera-Hellweg, Elizabeth Perez-Luna, Rogelio Villareal, Ernie and Bobbie Whiteman, los mártires de Highways, los Fast Würms, los post-Chicanos de Culture Clash, y la flotísima de Black Audio Film Collective.

• to my comadres, Marieta Bernstoff, Lourdes Grobet, Celeste Olalquiaga, Araceli Zúñiga, Mavis Bustamente, Tere Romo, Marta Vega, Judy Baca, María Eraña, Yolanda López, Mia Gonzalez, María Pineda, María Eliana Montaner, Liz Lerma Bowerman, Maruca Salazar, Carol Becker, and Nena Torres. They still have the political clarity we, the vatos peleoneros, have lost.

• to all the daring cultural organizers and friends who have taken the risk to support my work: Kim Chan, Claire Peeps, Julie Lazare, Marda Kirn, Norman Frisch, Gary Garrels, Carlos Tortolero, Susan Sillins, Steve Lavine, John Killacky, David White, Peter Taub, Joel Snyder, Alita Ringleno, and muy en particular to Lynn Schuette who gave me my first performance opportunities in the United States del Carajo.

• to the next generation, my beloved nephews, robo-raza members Ricardiaco, Carlitos, and Cristóbal, and the Chicano Secret Service, ni quién los pare...and of course, se me olvidaba, to the MacArthur Foundation. Thank you for the daily tacos and the new masks, mínimo.

Without these marvelous individuals and institutions, the contents of this book would be substantially different. Thanks to this tribe, I am not mad, in jail, or dead . . . yet.

G. G. P.

CONTENTS

I AM THEREFORE I CROSS

MY RATIONALE FOR CROSSING IS SIMPLE:

SURVIVAL + DIGNITY = MIGRATION − MEMORY

**GRAFFITI
(SAN DIEGO, 1983)**

INTRODUCTION

WHEN WE APPROACH A BORDER, the first thing that we worry about is how to cross it. A border tends to be a wall we can only cross if we have the necessary documents; it is a filter that is supposed to purify the passing flux. We can also approach a border wanting to transgress it, to cross it illegally, and to violate its rules. Whether we approach submissively with our passport and visa in hand, or as "wetbacks" who scurry silently, protected by the night, the border stands waiting for us to cross, or to detain us; but we are not supposed to live there. The border is a line that demands straightforward behavior; a red alarm lights if we "approximate it tangentially" (as in *irse por la tangente*), in the sense that this phrase can have in Spanish of cleverly evading or escaping trouble. The border is anathema to the ambiguity of people like Guillermo Gómez-Peña, who approximate borders tangentially as a way of life and a mode of expression.

This "tangential" attitude of Gómez-Peña is incredibly creative, and opens the doors of the imagination to a new sensibility; that of the exile, who, with a nomad's eyes, discovers that this tangential approach to the border allows him to see things that were once hidden. To begin with, that tangential look quickly discovers that Latin America does not end at the U.S. border; rather, Latino culture has penetrated the Anglo world. In the United States, the "Hispanic" sector of society, of the economy, of politics, and of culture is enormous and exercises considerable influence. Mexican nationalism has traditionally refused to recognize this, since the Mexicanization of life in the United States is more likely to be seen as the Americanization of the Mexicans.

The tangential look also confronts the commonly held idea that the border represents a permanent danger. The border is perceived by some as a constant source of contamination and a threat to Mexican identity. And yet, the mere existence of the border is what permits us to maintain tense nationalist passions. It allows, shall we say, for Mexicans to maintain a permanent state of alert before threats from outside. This state of alert, however, is clearly only symbolic, since the demographic reality of thousands of Mexicans who come and go across the border (more go than come) generates a sociocultural process of *mestizaje* and symbiosis that no nationalist discourse can stop. This cultural process has been defined by Guillermo Gómez-Peña as the borderization of the world. From his perspective, the border is no longer a wound whose pain serves to reaffirm identity, but rather a place where Anglos and Latinos confront one another. That corresponds to the pious medieval and Christian belief that it was necessary to deal with temptation and suffering to reaffirm faith. I do not think that, in terms of culture, we should be alarmed by what happens at the border. What is usually called an "Americanization" or a "Mexicanization" of border life is not an especially damaging or dangerous process. As an anthropologist, I cannot conceive of a border territory between two cultures where processes of transculturation do not occur. Any intent to impede this is, in the best of cases, utopian. When some gringos get alarmed by the Mexicanization of the border, they are having the same conservative and reactionary impulse as Mexican chauvinists. Life on the border, far from being a danger, could be the starting point of the *gringostroika* that has been called for since the fall of the Berlin Wall. Gómez-Peña's "tangential look" proves that if a continental grassroots movement that advocates the complete economic and cultural reform of U.S. capitalism does not exist, then it is time for it to begin.

Guillermo Gómez-Peña invites us to live on the border, to convert ourselves into permanent exiles, into nostalgic and melancholic beings, and to undergo the dangers that take us to the discovery of the infected wound. But this is not a rare condition; today, a mass of exiles extends itself throughout the world. In growing numbers, migrant populations, who tend to be escaping political and economic miseries, form an anonymous group in many countries of the world. It seems to me that, in the end, those who live a multicultural condition due to directly political reasons also form part of this immense wave of nomads who live a singular kind of exile; that is, the millions of Latin Americans, Asians, and Africans residing in Europe and the United States. It is true that the flux that obeys political rationales chooses strange routes, at times against the current, not always leading to the most developed regions of the West. There have also been fluxes of Europeans who have escaped "civilization" to look for new spaces of freedom in various parts of the world. The disintegration of the socialist bloc is also provoking particular forms of migration and exile.

There is something medieval in the condition of the exile, and of the migrant. For him/her, the political borders and military blockades have a different meaning. Because of this, I believe that the words of Hugo de Saint Victor have a special meaning for exiles: "A man who finds his homeland sweet is still a tender beginner; he to whom every soil is as his native one is already strong, but the perfect man is he who finds that the whole world is like a foreign land." Mystical temptation frequently attracts migrants and exiles, since it is an invitation to walk with the permanent certainty that we will never find what we are looking for. Nonetheless, we cannot stop our route along the dangerously tangential line, in search of a land called poetry. Rene Char defines it as follows: "In poetry one no longer lives in the place one left, one creates only that which one leaves behind, and one does not achieve duration without destroying time." That is the territory of an immense cohort of vagabonds or permanent exiles to which Guillermo Gómez-Peña belongs.

ROGER BARTRA
Translated by Coco Fusco

WARRIOR FOR GRINGOSTROIKA

A BINATIONAL
PERFORMANCE PILGRIMAGE

Excerpted from my performance diaries, this text chronicles two decades of projects, trips, and social and cultural phenomena that shaped the consciousness and sensibility of my generation. Though I chose to order the text in a somewhat chronological manner, the reader must keep in mind that some of the projects I talk about took place simultaneously and were related conceptually to other projects that were also taking place at the same time in different cities of the Southwest and the East Coast of the U.S.A.

I don't claim to have "the true story." Like any writer, I chose to highlight certain facts which I considered paradigmatic. There are probably many serious omissions, and I hope that those of you who were omitted will forgive me.

I WAKE UP AS A MEXICAN in U.S. territory. With my Mexican psyche, my Mexican heart, and my Mexican body, I have to make intelligible art for American audiences who know very little about my culture. This is my daily dilemma. I have to force myself to cross a border, and there is very little reciprocity from the people on the other side.

I physically live between two cultures and two epochs. I have a little house in Mexico City, and an apartment in New York, separated from each other by a thousand light-years in terms of culture.

I also spend time in California. As a result, I am a Mexican part of the year, and a Chicano the other part. I cross the border by foot, by car, and by airplane. I also cross the border in my dreams and my friendships.

When I am on the Mexican side, I have strong artistic connections to Latin American urban pop culture and ritual traditions that are centuries old. When I am on the U.S. side, I have access to high technology and specialized information. When I cross back to Mexico, I get immersed in a rich counterculture: the post-earthquake movements of opposition. When I return to the United States, I am part of the inter- and cross-cultural thinking emerging from the interstices of the U.S. ethnic milieus.

My journey goes not only from South to North, but from the past to the future, from Spanish to English, and from one side of myself to another. I walk the fibers of this transition in my everyday life, and I make art about it.

My experience is not unique by any means. Thousands of artists of color in the United States, Canada, and Europe are currently crossing different kinds of borders. And as they do it, they are making a new kind of art, an art of fusion and displacement that shatters the distorting mirrors of the "Western avant-garde."

El Half and Half

I am a writer in Mexico, where writers are respected and listened to, and a performance artist in the United States, where writers are marginalized. My performance art is above all a strategy of social communication and an exercise in cultural translation.

My activities as a cultural commentator and my performance work have always influenced each other. My theoretical voice is more balanced and logical, or at least that's what I think. My performance voice is frantic and fractured. They often invade one another.

Both my writings and my performances have an epic tone, for I believe that the contemporary Latin American experience in the United States, framed by diaspora, economic despair, police harassment, cultural exclusion, and aesthetic misunderstanding is of epic dimensions.

I want to articulate the ever-changing parameters of my multiple communities, but always from a multidimensional perspective, the border perspective, the only one I know. I crisscross

from the past to the present, from the fictional to the biographical. I fuse prose and poetry, sound and text, art and literature, political activism and art experimentation. As a result I find myself working with hybrid genres and interdisciplinary formats. My works are simultaneously essays and manifestos, performances and social chronicles, bilingual poems and radio or video pieces. In them I try to exercise all the freedom that my two countries have denied me.

The Womb

I was born in September of 1955, at the Spanish Hospital in a Jewish quarter of Mexico City, the most densely populated metropolis on earth.

I was the darkest of three children. Darkest both in terms of skin complexion and personality. My father was darker than I, a gallant sportsman with a quintessential *mestizo* look. My mother was as white as can be. She looked like a Spanish *doña*, though she was filled with Mexican tenderness. Having a red-haired sister and a blond brother, I always felt slightly odd, for I had to be "twice as clean and well dressed" to look *decente*.

I attended Jesuit schools. There I became aware of skin privilege. *Los niños bien* (the nice boys) were fair-skinned and European-looking. And *los nacos* (the sleazy ones) were darker and shorter. As a mestizo, I was a bit of both—*cafe con leche*, let's say.

Racism in modern-day Mexico is not like the militant versions found in the United States or South Africa. Rather it is a by-product of the country's inflexible social structure. Nonetheless, as a teenager I knew that my looks weren't totally acceptable. The mother of my teenaged *novia*, Adriana, once said: "Guillermo is not *feíto* (ugly), but unfortunately he is *prietito* (dark)." I still carry that thorn in my heart, and the United States has infected the wound.

COLONIAL DREAMS/HIPITECA DAYS

Like other Mexicans of my generation, I had to face three forms of colonialism. Spain was present in the skin privilege of the upper class and in the petty conservatism of the middle class. France was a plague that afflicted the "high" cultural scene. Until the early 1970s, young Mexican writers had to: a) learn French, b) read European writers, and c) one day go to Paris to be initiated. I chose not to do any of the three.

U.S. culture was perhaps the most blatant colonial presence. Over eighty percent of the TV programs and films, and more than half of the music on the radio were made in the United States. We also acquired U.S. culture regularly in the form of canned goods, toiletries, clothing, electrical appliances, and cars. My friends and I knew more about the United States than perhaps many American teens. We heard rock and roll all day long and devoured bad Spanish translations of John Dos Passos, Henry Miller, and the Beat poets. From the outside, we saw American culture as a quest for sexual and spiritual liberation. And to come North became a kind of generational obsession, a rite of passage to modernity. Modernity, like utopia, was always located in the North.

I returned to Mexico from my first trip to California in 1968 with four suitcases filled with hippie clothes, posters, porno magazines, Cream, Country Joe McDonald, and Animals albums. I decorated my room like a psychedelic parlor, which gave me special status with my friends. I became a *hipiteca*, perhaps the very first border character I ever internalized. My neighborhood *cuates* and I formed a weekend rock band. We developed an eclectic repertoire that included *boleros*, *rancheras*, and British pop songs in *Ingleñol*. We sang in this made-up English to impress the *chavas*.

When I entered *preparatoria* (junior high), I began to travel extensively throughout the Mexican countryside, and on these trips with my family and friends, I slowly discovered the labyrinthine essence and many souls of my culture. From the mulatto tropics of the Gulf to the ancient Indian cities of Yucatan, Chiapas, and Oaxaca, and from the colonial towns of central Mexico to the immense northern deserts, I discovered a multiplicity of Mexicos and Mexicans, each existing in a different time, each framed by different cultural and ethnic parameters, each speaking to a different part of my psyche.

THE PUZZLE OF IDENTITY

I entered university in 1973. At the Facultad de Filosofia y Letras, I underwent a fanatical conversion to Marxism—but an ultra-nationalistic brand. I became intolerant of anything not Mexican or not working-class. I consumed only national food, literature, music, philosophy, and political thought. I joined the already agonizing student movement and broke with my social class, including my beloved family, but the dogmatic behavior of my older *compañeros*, sinking sadly in the last waves of the student movement, soon persuaded me to open a very different door.

I immersed myself in the much-touted "inner search" that led my generation to investigate witchcraft, ritual drugs, Yaqui and Huichol philosophy, *conchero* dance (a syncretic tradition of ritual dance), Zen, and the combined and largely misinterpreted teachings of Castañeda, Ouspensky, Gurdjieff, and Krishnamurti. I became "Krishnahuatl" and my new objective was "to step outside of society" in order to reach "the ultimate reality."

Fortunately, most of the shamans and "men of knowledge" I met during my "pilgrimage of power" didn't match my stereotype. Far from being austere and contemplative, they were courageously engaged in social reality, and their ritual practices took place in specific political contexts, such as the struggles for land or human rights. They were also rowdy, quite theatrical, and didn't regard mass culture as a threat to their "authenticity."

The harshest but most important lesson I learned during those years was the realization that my Mexican *soledad* (in Spanish there is only one word to describe loneliness and solitude) was produced by social crisis and political ignorance—not by metaphysical orphanhood—and that my true spirituality as a Latin American could only be realized in the accidental terrain of sociopolitical interactions. Slowly, the biographical threads of my troubled adolescence began to intertwine into a somewhat coherent pattern. Words like crisis, rupture, fragmentation, and pluralism became part of my existential vocabulary.

At the end of that painful journey, I was finally able to complete the puzzle of my identity. Being a contemporary Mexican means being crucified by the East, the West, the North, and the South. We are a syncretic blend of Amerindian and European cultures, of pre-industrial traditions and imported technology—immersed in the past but always welcoming the new, the other, the foreign, no matter how dangerous it is. (Didn't we welcome Hernán Cortés, Maximilian of Hapsburg, and the American multinationals? Don't we still welcome all tourists, impresarios, and burnouts from the "industrialized" countries?) Our sensibility is the sum of these contradictions.

INVOLUNTARY POSTMODERNISM
Mexico City is the "postmodern" city par excellence. Walking from neighborhood to neighborhood is like traveling from continent to continent and vertically from one epoch to another. Pre-Columbian ruins stand alongside colonial Span-

ish and neoclassical French architecture. Houses built in different epochs during the past four centuries stand next to crystal skyscrapers hosting corporations and banks. Indian markets and video-discotheques are within walking distance of one another, and somehow it all makes sense.

Art in Mexico City is no less hybrid and unselfconsciously postmodern. The sounds of regional folk music coexist on the radio with classical European music and rock and roll in both English and Spanish. On any given day, one can witness an Indian dance ceremony at the zócalo, and then walk to a nearby theatre or gallery to attend a contemporary art event from Europe or North or South America.

Despite all this, the official culture provides us with an idealized and static version of who we were (heroic Indians) and who we are (modernized *mestizos*), which denies the rampant syncretism of everyday reality. From Aztec to post-punk, all styles, eras, and cultural expressions are intertwined in this mega-pastiche called "el D.F." (Mexico City), and those of us who grew up in such a context developed a vernacular postmodern sensibility with cross-cultural fusion at its core. Through the prism of this sensibility, past and present, pop culture and high culture, politics and aesthetics, rural and urban realities, pre-Columbian rite and Catholicism are perceived as either logical dualities belonging to the same time and place, or as overlapping realities.

Most Anglo-Americans have to learn postmodernism as theory because their cultural experience is not marked by growing within and across multiple cultural strata. Their knowledge of Native American culture is distant and abstract, and their attraction to African American and Latino art is selective and temporary. In fact, the relationships that Anglo-Americans establish with their cultural "others" are either of sponsorship, ventriloquism, messianism, or voyeurism, but very seldom of total immersion or uninterrupted dialogue.

Today in 1991, the United States still doesn't have a critical discourse to understand and explain its own *mestizaje*. In Mexico, we are immersed in syncretism, and our survival skills to move laterally and vertically into the cultural other are quite developed. We have no other choice. The other exists within us. This multiple otherness within constitutes the very spinal cord of our personal and collective biography. It is only until we cross the border that we face "the other outside," thus becoming the outside other for Anglo culture. When we cross the border, our art becomes the double mirror that reflects this painful dynamic: Mexico-in-the-United States, the United States-in-Mexico, and us in between.

THE GRUPOS VS. THE MAFIA

The Mexican cultural apparatus is both extraordinarily developed and oppressive. The infrastructure and public space available for artists and intellectuals to participate in national debates and shape public opinion is larger than in most countries, yet the rules of the game are very tight. *Compadrismo, influencias,* and complicated cocktail rites are but a few of the many steps that one must undertake to become part of the powerful intellectual mafias.

I have always been socially clumsy, impatient, and confrontational, and since my early incursions onto the terrain of the intelligentsia, I have realized that it is no place for me. As a young writer sneaking into exclusive parties and *tertulias* (literary gatherings), I would always end up condemning a sacred cow or spilling wine in a potential publisher's lap.

Fortunately, my friends were like me.

We studied literature and linguistics at the Universidad Nacional Autónoma de México and belonged to several literary workshops; yet our true literary activities were on the streets of Mexico City, which we considered our playground and laboratory. Our cultural avatars were the interdisciplinary *grupos* who were using the streets as "alternative spaces." Groups such as Proceso Pentágono, Suma, and Peyote y la Compañia, among others, produced irreverent *acciones* (performances), installations, and *pintas* (impromptu murals) inspired by urban pop culture and oppositional politics. They provided the only existing context for the overlapping of genres and métiers. Their blend of experimentation and activism was much closer to my everyday reality than the ontological explorations of the colonized literary circles I knew. Though the *grupos* were practically written out of contemporary Mexican art history, they represent the true zeitgeist of the 1970s, and without them, there would be no experimental art in Mexico today.

ANARQUÍA SOCIEDAD ANÓNIMA

I belonged to a very informal young group with the pompous name of Anarquía S.A.. Inspired by the notion of "interdisciplinary troublemaking," we made performance poetry, ritual happenings, and atonal music following the guttural dictates of sexual impulse, political bravado, and anticlericalism.

Mari Cármen Copani, a young Argentine writer, and I were dissidents within the group because of our extremist temperaments. We simulated assaults on the metro. We disrupted conventional poetry readings and lectures with absurdist questions, and showed up at public places in disguise. Once I entered the church of San Agustín dressed as a transvestite, arm in arm with Mari Cármen, who was dressed as a pregnant nun. Another time we drove around the parochial town of Tehuixtla without clothes. And whenever we saw a group of men hanging out at the park or outside a cantina, Mari Cármen would step out of the car to dance an epileptic *cumbia*. As the villagers began to react, we would drive away.

We were young and extremely dissatisfied with the aesthetic protectionism and the cultural solemnity of Mexico. I believe it was 1975 and we didn't know we were doing "performance art." We never imagined that our funky social experiments were part of an international movement with a registered tradition, an infrastructure, and a theoretical framework. Of course, we never bothered to document our work. All there is left from those days is a bunch of unpublished poems, snapshots, and diaries that haven't been opened.

THE DAY MY UMBILICAL CORD GOT INFECTED

The late 1960s in Mexico were a time of diaspora. Many experimental artists who felt suffocated by the inflexible monodisciplinary structures of the official culture left the country in search of aesthetic freedom and spread throughout Europe and the United States. Ulysses Carrión (RIP) went to Amsterdam where he started an alternative space called the In-Out Center; Felipe Ehrenberg went to England, where he co-founded the legendary *Beau Geste* alternative press and participated in the Fluxus movement.

In the late 1970s, my permanently unsatisfied friends and I departed following the footprints of our older *compadres*. I chose California, because I had always been more anti-European than anti-American, and because I wanted to embrace the Chicano experience, which at the time was completely mythical to Mexicans. A child of the Mexican crisis, I crossed the border in 1978 and something broke inside of me, forever. . .

Crossing the border meant much more than

having to learn English or eat bad food. For the first time I had to confront Protestant ethics, pragmatism, hyper-individualism, and racism on a daily basis; for the first time in my life I was truly alone and scared, without a family, a community, or a language. Utopia began to evaporate.

This abrupt confrontation with otherness triggered many processes inside of me, the most significant being the exploration of the conflictive relationship between my Mexican past and my U.S. present; my Latin American identity and my new Chicano reality. Again, this process found its most effective and organic format in performance.

My early solo performances in California reflected the pain of the departure and the indescribable loneliness of the immigrant. Once I spent twenty-four hours in a public elevator wrapped in a batik cloth. In many ways, this performance was my American birth rite. I was kicked, fondled, and cursed by strangers, and peed on by a dog. I only spoke once during the entire performance. When someone verbally threatened to stab me, I began to scream in Spanish until he ran away. I ended up being thrown into a trash can by security guards. Another time I brought my audience to the edge of Interstate 5 and screamed at the cars to stop and "save me from cultural shipwreck." When I was first busted by the California police for "looking suspicious," meaning for being Mexican, my response was to do a performance in which I burned a photo of my mother while screaming at the top of my lungs over the Los Angeles skyscrapers, *"Madre, házme regresar a la placenta!/* Mother, take me back to the womb!" I was desperately trying to find my place and my voice in a country with a long tradition of "Mexiphobia."

Performance gave me a vocabulary and a syntax to express the processes of loss, rupture, and deterritorialization I was undergoing. And through my performance practices, I was able to begin connecting with others who were experiencing a similar drama.

A MEXICAN LOST TRIBE

By coming to El Norte I paid a high price for my curiosity. I unknowingly became part of a lost tribe. As citizens of nowhere or, better said, of everywhere, we were condemned to roam around the foggy and unspecific territory known as border culture. Today, a decade later, we still haven't been able to "return" completely.

Despite the fact that I spend long periods of time in Mexico City, still write regularly for Mexican publications, and maintain a close dialogue with many artists and writers from "the center," in Mexico City I am referred to as "Chicano." The anthologies and festivals of Mexican culture rarely include my work because "Guillermo, you live on the other side." And to live on this side still implies a form of betrayal. When I go back to give a talk, I have to do so as a Chicano. My Mexican brothers have managed to turn me into the other, along with the 25 million Mexicans spread throughout the United States.

Paradoxically, some Chicanos still have a hard time considering me a "Chicano," either because I wasn't born in Aztlán, I didn't participate in the political struggles of the 1960s and 1970s, or I still have an accent that gives away my *chilango* (a derogative term for a Mexico City native) upbringing.

I have learned not to get hurt or waste my time demanding to be included in the nationalistic maps of Mexican or Chicano culture. I have learned to accept the advantages and disadvantages of being a "border citizen," which means I am always the other, but I get to choose my identity. Depending on the context, I can be a Mexican, a post-Mexican, a Chicano, a *chica-lango* (half-chicano and half-*chilango*), a Latin American, a trans-American, or an American—in the widest sense of the term. When I go to Europe, things get even more complicated. In England I am considered "Black" along with all Indians, Pakistanis, and Afro-Caribbeans. In France I am often mistaken for Algerian; and in Belgium, Switzerland, and Germany, I ipso facto become a Turk, a Greek, or a Yugoslavian Gypsy.

One thing I know for sure: my identity, like that of my contemporaries, is not a monolith but a kaleidoscope; and everything I create, including this text, contains a multiplicity of voices, each speaking from a different part of my self. Far from being mere postmodern theory, this multiplicity is a quintessential feature of the Latino experience in the United States.

CALIFORNIA, FORNICARE SIN MEMORIA

When I first arrived in Los Angeles to study post-studio art at the California Institute of the Arts, I felt strangely happy in a context that encouraged experimentation without restrictions, yet I was appalled by the prevailing ethnocentrism. The main focus of the art department was New York conceptual art. And, despite the fact that East L.A., the largest Chicano barrio in the United States, was only forty-five minutes away, and that the Mexican border was only two and a half hours away, I was never able to engage in an intelligent conversation about Chicano or Latin American culture that went beyond the purely anecdotal.

Like many U.S. campuses, Cal Arts was geographically and culturally isolated from the rest of the country, not to mention the world. In the absence of overt social crisis and political immediacy, most art students were involved in their personal process, a notion foreign to third-world artists, yet so prevalent in the United States at the time. This personal process was restricted to the realms of sexual and psychological crisis, family hatred, and technological idolatry.

I felt like a Mexican Alice in Wonderland. The students practiced nudity in the swimming pool, yet very few were sexually active. The visiting-artist program was very active, but only a handful of non-white intellectuals visited the school while I was there. Liberalism and coolness were on the surface, yet racism and isolationism lay underneath.

In this totally bizarre (in the eyes of a Mexican) context, I became an outcast, and naturally gravitated toward other outcasts who were either foreign students or "minorities." We called ourselves "The Tribe of the Inflamed Eyelids" (or the fiery pupils), and our main sport was to denounce ethnocentrism.

In those days, the need to survive culturally in an alienating environment such as Cal Arts made me create performances in which I overstated my *Mexicanidad*, my marginality, my otherness. If it wasn't for the help of some marvelous teachers and L.A. artists who graciously explained to me the bizarre topography of U.S. culture, I would probably have decided to return to Mexico.

THE OTHER UNITED STATES
In 1979 I began venturing into the inner city, in search of my incipient Chicano identity.

I wasn't exactly welcomed by the East L.A. Chicanos. Distrustful, militant, and anti-intellectual, they had no time for an arrogant *chilango* hipster like me. But I was stubborn enough to persist. I badly needed a *flota* (community) that could save me from cultural starvation.

My ambassador to East L.A. was my friend, Chicano filmmaker Juan Garza. He invited me to ASCO performances, low-rider car shows, bilingual poetry readings, and Day of the Dead parades. It was there that I began to look at the United States with different eyes. With my new eyes, I saw this country no longer as the mythical all-white mighty power that Mexicans fear so much, but as a multiracial/multilingual complex with myriad points of view. This realization gave me the courage to stay and the desire to participate in the making of a culture that included my vision.

Chicanismo provided me with the intellectual, political, and artistic means to begin my process of "reterritorialization" and to eventually regain my lost citizenship. I no longer thought of myself as a foreigner, but as a citizen of the other America. Since then, *Califas* (not California), and *Aztlán* (not the U.S. Southwest) have become part of my cultural topography, a conceptual continent I call *Arteamérica*.

TRANSCULTURAL ORPHANS
In 1981, choreographer Sara-Jo Berman and I founded Poyesis Genética performance troupe, a fluctuating core of eight to ten artists from various disciplines and ethnic backgrounds, all studying at Cal Arts.

Poyesis was my first conscious attempt to make art in a culturally pluralistic, collaborative, and interdisciplinary mode. The original objective was, and I quote an early press release, "to create an intercultural space in which to fuse and juxtapose the various artistic and performing traditions brought by the members." Perhaps the only thing we had in common was our willingness to step outside of our cultures and to experiment. In a sense we were a bunch of rejects of monoculture.

During the first year we developed a sui generis performance style that resulted from "the blending of Mexican *carpa* (a tradition of urban popular theatre), magical realism, kabuki, and U.S. multimedia." Where else but in California could this lunatic pastiche have happened?

Though the scripts were written by me, the images and movement were conceived collectively through long discussions that would often take place in more than three languages. Most scripts

1981 "THE BIRTH OF POYESIS GENÉTICA"

The neo-tribalism of Poyesis Genética Troupe is expressed in this scene from their first performance.

(From the archives of Poyesis Genética).

were based on the following metafiction: Mister Misterio, a Mexican detective/poet, and his friend Salome Zentit, a burned-out ballerina, underwent a series of cross-cultural adventures. They belonged to the Tribe of the Fiery Pupils, an international group of radicals devoted to the dismantling of a monocultural order. Each performance was a different episode in the Misterio/Salome saga, and their friends and enemies included hybrid characters such as the Wrestler Shaman, Multimedia Pachuco, an Aztec princess who worked as a cabaret chanteuse, and an androgynous Maori warrior who sang opera.

Before every performance we underwent a series of elaborate ritual steps to reach a trancelike state that included fasting, chanting, breathing exercises, and ritual dinners. We built multimedia altars with a video monitor as main icon. These altars functioned as both set design and nerve center of the ceremonial space. Onstage, we practiced ritual nudity and slow-motion movement counterpointed by film and slide projections. According to one critic, the result was a kind of "techno-magical realism, that contrasted with the prevailing minimalist performance style" of the time. More than techno-magical realists, I think we were a bunch of orphans trying to come to terms with a new culture, not quite ours yet.

RETERRITORIALIZATION

Poyesis died and was resuscitated two times under extremely different circumstances.

In 1982, Sara-Jo and I dismantled the California group and blindly headed for Europe, where we built a transient version of Poyesis. From the Parisian lofts of Latin American exiles to the streets of Basel and Zurich; from German alternative spaces to the Mexican Embassy of Bern, we fine-tuned our performance and survival skills.

The Mexican financial crack of 1982 caught me in Brussels with my pants down and a couple thousand pesos that disintegrated in my pocket. I phoned Mexico City, and my father told me to go to the Tijuana/San Diego border region and wait for better times. I never imagined that the wait was going to be a decade long.

In 1983, Poyesis moved to *la frontera* under the protection of Sushi Gallery and the Casa de la Cultura de Tijuana. On the border, Poyesis found a mega-context of syncretism and cultural fusion that seemed ideal for the work we were doing. At the border we found marvelous collaborators like Luke Theodore Morrison (RIP), ex-member of the Living Theatre, Chicana performance artist Yareli Arismendi, and Mexican journalist Marco Vinicio González who were to become my co-conspirators in many future adventures.

Marco Vinicio, then sub-director of the Casa de la Cultura, originally envisioned creating the first border performance art milieu. Besides hosting Poyesis, he invited dancers, musicians, and performance artists from Mexico City to collaborate with Chicano poets and *teatristas*. For a year and a half, the Casa became the largest alternative space on the border. Because of the total absence of a performance-art tradition in Tijuana, we were regarded by the local authorities as "a bunch of weirdos, *chilangos*, and *pochos* (a derogative term for Chicano; he who bastardizes the Spanish language)." And we did our best to honor this title. In 1985, after the binational production of *Ocnoceni*, the third Poyesis group slowly faded into the newly formed Border Arts Workshop.

THE ARTIST AS BINATIONAL DIPLOMAT

My early years in the border region (1983-1985) were wonderfully complicated. I was earning my living as a journalist for Mexican and Chicano newspapers, and I was also trying to keep Poyesis alive, performing on both sides of the border. *La Prensa de San Diego* was paying me fifty dollars per week as editor of the cultural section of the paper, and *La Opinión* (Los Angeles) was offering me seventy-five dollars for a twelve-page interview or essay. Since at that time no one was interested in multiculturalism, Poyesis was mostly performing for free. Money was scarce but the utopian spirit of border culture kept me going. In order to be able to eat decently, I decided to become a food critic. With the company of hungry friends, I "reviewed" three or four different restaurants a week, until I got caught.

With the help of collaborators Marco Vinicio González and María Eraña, I turned my home into an alternative information center named Border Inc. We provided an incredible amount of free binational services, such as translating important news items and essays and sending them to the other country, and linking groups of artists, intellectuals, and journalists from Mexico and the United States interested in dialogue with the other side of the border. We also developed several binational arts projects that challenged the existing separatist notions about border culture.

In 1984, my *compadre* Marco Vinicio and I started a bilingual radio show on KPBS, entitled "Border Dialogues." The idea was "to gather people from both sides of the border to discuss common problems in the territories of education, politics, and art." For two years, we were able to invite people as diverse as Mexican performance artist Marcos Kurtycz, Chicana poet Gina Valdez, and border/human-rights activists Víctor Clark and Jose Luis Pérez Canchola. We literally handed our guests an hour of radio time to say whatever they pleased, and to use the radio format as creatively as they could. The program reached Ensenada, Tecate, Tijuana, and San Diego County, and the transcripts were published by the newspapers *La Opinión* and *El Mexicano* (Tijuana).

These radio dialogues gave us a clear sense of the impact we could have as border diplomats working independently, and triggered many projects in other media.

A PAINFUL PAUSE

I was working as performance coordinator for the fifteenth anniversary of the Centro Cultural de la Raza (San Diego) when the Mexico City earthquake occurred. It was September of 1985 and artist David Avalos gave me the news: part of my beloved city had literally crumbled and there were no telephone lines to verify the dimensions of the tragedy. My friend, poet Rubén Medina, and I went to Tijuana and got on the first plane to Mexico City we could find. The coming days were the most convulsive of my life. First I had to face the physical and emotional disaster (which I won't describe, for others have already done so), then I realized that it was up to each of us as children of the city to rebuild it. Everybody I knew was involved in some emergency task such as digging the wounded out from the debris or transporting medicine and food. I formed a brigade with my neighbors and nephews and we carried coffins for a week. My nephew Ricardo, who was twelve at the time, would tell me, "Tío, just don't look down. Look at the sky as you walk."

Mexican artists learned a harsh lesson: in times of disaster, the function of art becomes strictly utilitarian. Conceptual artist Felipe Ehrenberg, whose work as activist and chronicler was instrumental during the reconstruction process, put it very well: "If you are a visual artist, you donate your work for fundraising. If you are a writer or a singer, you try to heal with the word. If you know how to organize people, that becomes your art."

I don't know of any Mexican artist, writer, or activist whose work wasn't profoundly affected by the quake. A new art and a new political energy arose from the ruins and ashes of the biggest city on earth. The objective was to reconstruct two cities: the city inside each of us and the one we all shared. The trauma that we experienced continues to surface in our work. For my contemporaries, inside and outside Mexico, the 1985 earthquake has forever become an existential landmark, a generational parameter, and a key symbol of our artistic languages.

BREAKING THE LINE

In early 1986 Marco Vinicio and I began to publish *The Broken Line/La Línea Quebrada,* a bilingual/experimental magazine that was instrumental in defining a border aesthetic. A direct descendent of the legendary *El Corno Emplumado* (The Plumed Horn)—published in Mexico City during the 1960s by Margaret Randall and Sergio Mondragón—and a twin project of *La Regla Rota* (The Broken Rule)—published simultaneously, also in Mexico City, by Rogelio Villareal and Mongo—*The Broken Line* helped to restore the fragile axis of thought between Mexico City and California. We must remember that in the mid-1980s, the relationship between Mexicans and Chicanos was still marked by fear, resentment, and distrust.

Printed in Tijuana and distributed binationally from San Diego, the first issue caused us all kinds of problems with the Mexican cultural bureaucracy, who stupidly saw our call for binational dialogue as "integrationist" and "pro-American." Twice we were told to "cool off." Marco Vinicio, who lived in Tijuana, was blacklisted and never found a job there again. Some members of the Tijuana intelligentsia were also extremely antagonistic toward the project. They couldn't accept the idea of two *chilangos* attempting to explain border culture without consulting them. They felt they had exclusivity on the topic.

To our surprise, the Mexico City newspapers supported our border rebellion. The daily *Uno-Mas-Uno* said that "there [were] no comparable art magazines in the country," and this gave us carte blanche to continue causing trouble.

From the beginning, *The Broken Line* was an undefinable object, equidistant from conceptual art, Latin American concrete poetry, and Chicano pop culture. It looked like something between a "cholo-punk magazine" and a slick book-art piece. And despite the fact that we only published 1,000 copies per issue, we managed to become important players at the table of negotiations for border culture, which at the time was mostly dominated by academicians. Our sloppy distribution actually helped to create an aura of countercultural inaccessibility. Those who had a magazine in their hands treasured it as a collector's item. People would copy it and pass it around. Political and artistic groups from both countries continually expressed solidarity with us. The prestigious Mexico City newspaper *La Jornada* reprinted our graphics and photos to illustrate articles on border and Chicano culture. Marco and I were asked to appear in symposia with pompous scholars who regarded the magazine as "cultural pornography." They loved it, but felt obliged to attack it for "lack of intellectual rigor," or for "creating an exotic view of the border area."

In 1987, Marco Vinicio moved to New York and other co-editors joined with me in the making (and breaking) of *La Línea*. Interdisciplinary artists Emily Hicks, Harry Polkinhorn, and César Espinosa and filmmaker Isaac Artenstein helped to co-edit different issues.

During those days, three important movements began to reshape our cultural cartography: Soviet glasnost, U.S. multiculturalism, and the Mexican Cardenista movement. They were strangely akin in the sense that all three promoted reform, diversification, and tolerance, and we tried to capture these impulses in the pages of the magazine.

The most ambitious *Broken Line* project was a limited edition of 500 silkscreened boxes, each containing a traveling art exhibit in multiple formats, including conceptual postcards, fictional maps, photos, punk and low-rider drawings, political cartoons, and performance-art documents. The premise was that "once the exhibit was over, the receiver/accomplice would send his/her box to another city/country to continue the chain." The "traveling BL" was shown in several countries including the United States, Mexico, Cuba, Guatemala, Brazil, Spain, France and Sweden— in the latter three, as part of the blockbuster exhibit *Les Demons des Anges/The Demons of Los Angeles*. In fact, the luxurious multilingual catalogue for the exhibit utilized many pages of *The Broken Line* as inserts. Again, the impulse behind this project was to find new and surprising ways to distribute border art with a minimum of resources, and from an independent perspective.

THE BORDER AS PERFORMANCE LABORATORY

Since the success of our first show at the Galería de la Raza in January of 1985, we knew that the Border Arts Workshop/El Taller de Arte Fronterizo (BAW/TAF) was a paradigmatic experiment. This success wasn't due to the quality of the artwork, but to the intercultural nature of the collaborative process. The sense of belonging to a larger cause had almost totally broken down in the 1980s, especially within the art world. And the perspective of an interdisciplinary group of artists from the United States and Mexico working together to develop models of binational cooperation and cross-racial dialogue was not just a romantic but a necessary idea.

We must remember that 1985 was a key year for the Chicano cultural movement. Institutions such as the Galería de la Raza (San Francisco), SPARC (Los Angeles), and the Centro Cultural de la Raza (San Diego) began a process of redefining their relationships with the larger society. This led to the shedding of separatism and the creation of intercultural alliances with other Latinos, as well as African Americans, Asian Americans, feminists, and gays.

BAW/TAF was an offspring of this impulse. Its original members included Chicanos David Avalos and Victor Ochoa, Trinidadian Jude Eberhard, Americans Michael Schnorr, Sara-Jo Berman, and Philip Brookman, and Mexicans Isaac Artenstein and myself. We proclaimed the border region our "intellectual laboratory" and immediately undertook action. We began gathering weekly to discuss human-rights violations by the border patrol, racist media depictions of Mexico and Mexicans, and U.S. policy toward the South. In these lengthy discussions, we developed an effective set of strategies to "broadcast" our point of view and to intervene directly in the social landscape of the border. Unlike the unimaginative methods of straight political groups, we utilized experimental art techniques and performance-derived practices to garner the attention of the media.

One of our early performances, entitled *End of the Line*, took place on October 12, 1986, at the intersection of Border Field State Park and Playas de Tijuana, right where the United States meets with Mexico at the Pacific. Dressed as "border stereotypes," members of the workshop and friends sat at a huge binational table bisected by the borderline. The Mexicans were in Mexican territory and the Chicanos and Anglos were on the U.S. side. We began to "illegally" hold hands and exchange food across the line. At one point we turned the table 360 degrees and entered "illegally" into each other's countries. The three carabelas of Columbus made out of flammable material were set on fire on the seascape. The Mexican media reported the event as news, and we became aware of the political power of site-specific performance. A cultural act emerging from such a politically charged site as the U.S./Mexico border carries much more weight and many more implications than similar gestures in the interior of either country.

In 1987, Artenstein, Eberhard, Brookman, and Berman left the group. They were later replaced by Emily Hicks, Robert Sanchez, Berta Jottar, and Rocio Weiss. Avalos eventually formed another collective with Louis Hock, Liz Sisco, James Luna, and Debora Small. We also benefited greatly from the ideas of Richard Lou who later joined the group.

Many other performance actions were staged at politically sensitive sites such as the border checkpoint, the legendary "soccer field," the San Diego Federal building (which hosts the offices of the INS), and on the streets of downtown San Diego. We also organized performance pilgrimages across the border and "tertulias" (town meetings) involving artists, journalists, and activists from both cities.

When Mexican political hero Superbarrio visited the border, we organized a performance town meeting with representatives from the various political, cultural, and media sectors of San Diego and Tijuana. We built a barbed-wire wrestling ring and impersonated border heroes such as *Supermojado*, *Superviviente*, *Chicanosaurio*, and *Saint Frida* (Kahlo). We welcomed Superbarrio and presented him with a pair of pliers "to cut the border fence."

We had to rely on the art world to protect our backs. And every now and then we would create installation pieces and performances in the safe environment of galleries and museums. Our strictly-art activities were important in the sense that they provided us with the space and safety to reflect on other contexts. We had a lot in common with ACT UP and the L.A.P.D. perfor-

mance troupe. We walked back and forth between the art world and the real world, and the prestige of the group was precisely built around these dynamics. By 1988 we were inundated with offers to create border projects in art spaces all over the country.

The process of popularization/institutionalization of BAW/TAF was so fast that we never had time for reflection. Suddenly individual members were being courted by important galleries, and major "institutions" began demagogically to utilize our ideas to organize festivals, symposia, and blockbuster shows that were opposite in nature to border culture.

In the summer of 1989, we developed our most ambitious project, *Border Axis,* at the Capp Street Project in San Francisco. Through fax machines, an 800-telephone line, and mail, we created a temporary network between twelve cities in three countries: the United States, Canada, and Mexico. We exchanged information with groups of artists and activists dealing with issues such as immigration, human rights, censorship, AIDS, and abortion. We also declared the space a Chicano cultural center and made all our resources available to local groups. We managed to temporarily turn a lily-white art space into an exciting multicultural community and media center. At the end of the summer, an accidental fire destroyed part of the installation, an omen for what was to come. The two-month project had been so massive in scale that it began to erode our health and interpersonal relations. We were at each other's throats, witnessing with perplexity and melancholy the exciting but uncontrollable monster we had created. Institutions across the country were willing either to invite us to attempt something similar or to undertake projects on their own inspired by our model. Even *Hispanic Business Magazine* and *People Weekly* magazine were chasing us around. It was time for serious reflection.

The group became ferociously divided. Michael felt that the group should take advantage of the momentum and continue to work. Others, including myself, felt that it was time to jump out of the wave before it hit the cliff. So we did. In November 1989, half of the members of BAW/TAF left the group. Robert Sanchez, Richard Lou, Berta Jottar, and Victor Ochoa stayed temporarily to work in the next two important projects: *Border Sutures*, a cross-country art journey zigzagging the U.S./Mexico border, and the legendary Venice Biennale piece, which, paradoxically, crowned the collective as an international superstar right when the original group was disbanding.

In late 1990, I believe, a new Border Arts Workshop was formed. I wish them my very best, for they have to face extremely serious obstacles.

The saddest thing about border culture is the fact that the intercultural collaborative process often reproduces the same conflicts as the larger society (racism, opportunism, desire/fear, cultural dependency, etc.). Today, after all these years, Chicanos and Mexicans are still unable to understand each other. We behave like members from a dysfunctional family divided by the borderline. The Tijuanenses are very resentful of the Anglos and *chilangos* (including myself) who are getting recognition for what they feel were also their ideas, and the Anglo-American women haven't fully worked out their differences with their Chicana and Mexican *comadres*. There is a lot of pain and misunderstanding; the border remains an infected wound. Perhaps the utopian spirit of the border project lies precisely in its impossibility.

Migrant Performance

Not everything can be expressed through group work. There are always certain issues that one can only deal with alone. And perhaps because of this, I have never stopped doing solo work. In my monologues I speak about the most delicate matters that pertain to my place in this world as a child of the Mexican diaspora in search of "the other Mexico." This country exists both beyond the national borders and inside my psyche.

In my solo work I don't have to depend on complex infrastructures and large numbers of people. I use a megaphone, a mike, and a ghetto blaster as my only technical support. I often perform behind a table filled with votive candles and ritual props. My props and costumes can easily fit in a suitcase. The portability of this type of work allows me to travel extensively. As I travel, I become a performance pilgrim, a migrant poet, a civilian diplomat, and a vernacular anthropologist. On these trips from coast to coast and from one country to another, I inevitably reproduce the migratory patterns of my people, the Mexicans outside Mexico. And the places and communities I come across become part of the cartography of my next piece.

As a rite of passage, my solo characters are often born by physically crossing the U.S./Mexico border checkpoint in costume. If the border patrol allows them into the country, that to me is a sign of their strength and raison d'être.

Dressed in an altar jacket and a rowdy wig, and carrying an old-fashioned bullhorn, *Border Brujo* first crossed the border on June of 1988. I/he spoke through ten different personae in four languages (Spanish, English, Spanglish, and tongues) about the fragmentation of the border self. I/he toured throughout northern Mexico, the United States, Canada, and Europe, performing indiscriminately at alternative spaces, museums, theatre festivals, political rallies, and community centers. And through him, I discovered the secrets to crossing the borders between cultures, communities, institutions, and territories of thought and action.

At the end of this exhausting saga, I received several surprises: the 1989 New York Bessie performance award, the Prix de la Parole at the International Theatre Festival of the Americas, a bleeding ulcer, and lots of trouble with the California police upon my return to the border. The San Diego district attorney managed to bust me three times within a period of two months. The charges weren't even that imaginative: I had stolen a radio—my own; I didn't respond to a court citation concerning a paternity suit from an unknown woman who claimed "she was the mother of three children (of mine)"; and I happened to have "the same name and address as, and look exactly like, a drug dealer" they were after. In the last bust, the marshals broke into my home, held me naked at gunpoint, right in front of my eight-month-old son and my ex-wife, and handcuffed me without ever reading me the Miranda Act. Thanks to my journalist friends who denounced these actions, and to a national radio show I did for "Crossroads," the harassment stopped. I discovered an interesting fact: performing political material outside the safe parameters of the art world can be as dangerous in the United States as it is in Latin America.

I finally buried the Brujo in February of 1990 at Life on the Water Theatre (San Francisco), and new characters emerged from his ashes. My *compadre* Isaac Artenstein made two films about him that are currently being distributed on video (*Border Brujo* and *The Son of Border Crisis*). The Brujo is stubborn. Despite my will, he still exists in virtual space, now as a "video-Brujo."

My new performance character, "the Warrior for Gringostroika," is a hybrid of a mariachi, a low-rider, and a disc jockey. He also has the superpower to unfold into other personae such as El Aztec High-Tech, El Untranslatable Vato, and El Charrollero. Like the Brujo, he irreverently uses pop culture and tourist artifacts as sacred objects, and a ghetto blaster as a musical instrument. He drinks from a rubber heart, plays with snakes, and boxes with chickens. He often appears on stage framed by hanging dead chickens, which to me are archetypal images of racism against Mexicans. (Up to the 1930s, Texas Rangers used to hang migrant workers, who are still referred to as *pollos* today.)

In my performance trilogy, *1992*, the Warrior appears as an "alternative chronicler of the re-discovery of America." In the Warrior's version of the re-discovery, the undocumented ghost of Christopher Columbus comes back to the "New World" to find that history is strangely repeating itself. The piece is a disnarrative meditation on the abrupt transition of decades, during which my personal biography as a Mexican-immigrant-gone-Chicano overlaps with the fictional biographies of my performance characters. Both narratives are intertwined with historical and political references as well as with poetical voices in various languages. In *1992*, I step away from the border as a specific site to begin looking elsewhere for "hybrid America," or for what Mexican artist Daniel Manrique calls "the universal barrio."

New Strategies

1989 and 1990 were confusing and terrifying years for humanity. From the Tiananmen Square massacre to the Baghdad genocide, we all felt the birth pains of the new millennium. Many borders were erased and others were instantaneously created. The amount, complexity, and intensity of the political changes in the world surpassed our capability to decodify them adequately. Everything seemed to be up for grabs: language, ideology, identity, religious faith, sexuality, and aesthetics. And in the middle of this *fin-de-siècle* earthquake, my colleagues and I were looking for a new place to speak from, and a new set of languages and metaphors capable of articulating our present crisis.

For me, those years meant the closing of a major chapter in my life. My beloved father died with the decade, right as my son Guillermo Emiliano was being born. With the fall of the Berlin Wall and the increased militarization of the U.S./Mexico border, the word "border" changed its meaning drastically. The Mexican government began to negotiate a Free Trade Agreement with Washington. And the United States far-right, in search of post-Cold War enemies, began to censor and de-fund art that expressed sexual and cultural difference. All this forced me to undertake a radical process of questioning my cultural parameters and aesthetic strategies. Since then, my main objectives have been to develop cross-racial collaborative models that are congruent with and reflective of what I call "the end-of-the-century society," and to create an art that promotes a new internationalism *ex centris,* one in which the nerve centers are located in the Third World within the First World, a conceptual place I call Arteamérica.

I have tried out various options, from recombining effective border-art strategies from my days with Poyesis Genética and the Border Arts Workshop to developing new ones that respond to the caprices and particularities of the present time. Some examples:

A. Performance as intercultural diplomacy. In July of 1990, I went to the Soviet Far East as part of a binational human-rights commission to exchange information with Soviet groups. We were one of the first "Western delegations" to visit the closed city of Vladivostok since the Stalin years. Unlike my colleagues, who presented either straight political data or decorative art objects as presents, I chose to present my art-as-information. With the help of two translators, I performed fragments of the first part of my *1992* trilogy-in-progress. I will never know exactly how well my attentive Russian audiences understood my Spanglish art but they seemed very touched. I also brought audio-tapes, slides, conceptual postcards, and issues of *The Broken Line.* These materials served as the basis for rich debates about the place of the artist in contemporary society. At the end of the trip one thing was clear to me: the artist as intercultural diplomat is able to cross many borders closed to solemn political activists.

B. Performance radio. Another useful strategy to disseminate radical ideas outside the safe parameters of the art world has been radio in all its forms—informational, conceptual, poetic, and performative. My involvement with (let's call it) performance radio stems from my collaborations with "The Territory of Art" radio-art series produced by Julie Lazare in Los Angeles, and with "Crossroads," the Miami-based national program. Elizabeth Perez-Luna, one of the best radio journalists in the country, and her husband Lenny Persky produce this extraordinary weekly audio-magazine that allows Latino, African, Asian, and Native American writers to have a national voice in a country where intellectuals and artists, confined to academic or alternative spaces, are only supposed to have opinions about their own métiers or their very specialized concerns. From 1987 to 1990 I covered U.S./Mexico relations for them, but always from the perspective of a performance artist. My shows had the "professional tone" of public radio, yet they were layered with poetic voices, strange musical juxtapositions, and sound effects. In fact, they very much resembled my live performances, with the difference that I got to present them for millions of people.

Last year, I was invited to participate in EDGE 90, the British Biennial of experimental art that took place in the northern city of Newcastle. Besides bringing my live performance work, I collaborated with two British radio pirates in a series of clandestine broadcasts from artists' lofts. For five days, we broadcast multilingual performance poems comparing the Chicano experience to that of British "minorities."

Even though pirate radio cannot take place in the United States (the radio airwaves are tightly controlled and legal punishment is exaggerated), I have managed to persuade some daring stations to simulate pirate interventions. One month before the NPR program "Heat" was taken off the air, John Hockenberry agreed to let me broadcast a fifteen-minute uncensored performance text dealing with racism and censorship in America. I have also persuaded some Pacifica stations to broadcast some of my performances live.

Another interesting experiment took place at a Columbia University radio station during the popular program "La Nueva Canción y Demás." Marco Vinicio González, journalist Maria Hinojosa, and I invited "all the undocumented *raza* from New York to call the studio, without identifying themselves by name, and share with us their border-crossing stories." To our surprise, dozens of newly arrived Mexicans, Caribbean Latinos, and Central Americans, protected by the anonymity of radio, called in and told, on the air, incredible stories of valor, pain, cruelty, and hope that no sociologist could have possibly obtained. Also, during the three-hour experiment, many of the callers exchanged information regarding social-service agencies, churches, and restaurants.

C. Cross-cultural/interdisciplinary collaboration. After my departure from BAW/TAF, I collaborated in a very ambitious project with writer and media artist Coco Fusco. Invited by Festival 2000 of San Francisco, we formed a temporary group with Latino and Anglo artists from both the East and West Coasts. We met in San Francisco several times during an entire year. The result of this dialogue was an installation at the Mexican Museum entitled *Norte/Sur*. From "au-thentic" pre-Columbian and colonial artworks juxtaposed with tourist art, to a multimedia altar composed of computer-generated projections, we attempted to articulate some of the intercultural dynamics that characterize the relationships between North and South, such as appropriation, creative expropriation, colonial dependency, vampirism, and nostalgic simulacra. The program stated: "America is not the United States. It is no longer the territory you imagine. Despite our hopes and fears, an incredible continental infection is spreading beyond our geo-political boundaries. Latin America lives and breathes in the United States and vice versa. What we buy, eat, watch, read, hear, and pay taxes for is transforming the North and the South into an intercultural terrain." In addition to the installation, we organized performances, lectures, and special tours, and Elizabeth Perez-Luna produced a half-hour radio version for binational distribution.

I have also developed collaborative projects with Chicano artists Robert Sanchez, Richard Lou, and Yareli Arismendi, Mexican rock singer Sergio Arau, Puerto Rican performance artist Papo Colo, and African American performance artist Keith Mason. Sharing resources, skills, and visions, artists from different cultural backgrounds and métiers can effectively negotiate a common ground that temporarily supersedes their/our differences. Though filled with hardships and dangers, this collaborative process is more necessary than ever before.

Carlos Fuentes insists that the political hope of our continent lies precisely in the cultural models developed by its imaginative writers and artists. The great challenge is how to transfer these models into the political arena. If we want to participate in the shaping of the future in a country that pushes us to the margins, we have to fight constantly for the right to have a public voice. But let's not mistake having a public voice for hype, or mistake marginality for ethics. Marginality can be a privilege for elite "Western bohemians," but to us it is a painful 500-year-old condition that must be overcome.

We must challenge the anachronistic myth that as "artists of color" we are *only* meant to work within the boundaries of our ethnic "communities." These boundaries have been imposed from above. Our place is the world in crisis and our community has multiplied exponentially. In the 1990s, I feel a strong kinship with everyone on this and other continents who is seeking new ways of interpreting the dangers and changes of the times: the border and Chicano artists; the Latinos, African Americans, Asian Americans, Native Americans, gays, and feminists who are willing to establish cross-cultural alliances with one another; the performance activists, the non-aligned intellectuals and journalists; the post-earthquake Mexico City rockers, and cartoonists; the post-colonial collectives from Europe; and the Latin American conceptual artists and writers who are so intelligently analyzing North/South relations. They all are my brothers and sisters of vision. They all are members of my conceptual nation. Their communities are also mine, and I hope my work will contribute to the creation of axes of thought and action among them.

I am currently working with Joe Lambert (San Francisco), Marco Vinicio González (New York), and others to create a trinational network of politicized artists and arts organizations—from Mexico, the United States, and Canada—interested in signing a "Free Art Agreement." The purpose is to exchange ideas and art (not consumer goods), and the means will be the creation of a trilingual arts magazine to be distributed simultaneously in all three countries along with the development of multiracial residencies that will bring together artists and thinkers from different cities.

The product of these ongoing gatherings will be a series of collaborative radio, video, and performance works that will challenge our restrictive notions of "national culture" and "Americaness."

For the moment, a major issue is haunting our consciousness: the need to demystify the quincentennial "celebration" of the alleged discovery of America, a blatant euphemism for the genocide that made "America" into the United States and Latin America into a subsidiary of Europe. It is my hope that 1992 will mark the end of many unnecessary binational pilgrimages and the beginning of a new society beyond Columbus, one in which Europeans and North Americans will no longer be our managers, bankers, law enforcers, and landowners, but our trustworthy partners.

[TO BE CONTINUED . . .]

CRITICAL TEXTS

DOCUMENTED/UNDOCUMENTED

I LIVE SMACK IN THE FISSURE between two worlds, in the infected wound: half a block from the end of Western civilization and four miles from the beginning of the Mexican/American border, the northernmost point of Latin America. In my fractured reality, but a reality nonetheless, there cohabit two histories, languages, cosmologies, artistic traditions, and political systems which are drastically counterposed. Many "deterritorialized" Latin American artists in Europe and the United States have opted for "internationalism" (a cultural identity based upon the "most advanced" of the ideas originating out of New York or Paris). I, on the other hand, opt for "borderness" and assume my role: my generation, the *chilango* (slang term for a Mexico City native), who came to "El Norte" fleeing the imminent ecological and social catastrophe of Mexico City, gradually integrated itself into otherness, in search of that other Mexico grafted onto the entrails of the et cetera . . . became Chicano-ized. We de-Mexicanized ourselves to Mexi-understand ourselves, some without wanting to, others on purpose. And one day, the border became our house, laboratory, and ministry of culture (or counterculture).

Today, eight years after my departure from Mexico, when they ask me for my nationality or ethnic identity, I can't respond with one word, since my "identity" now possesses multiple repertories: I am Mexican but I am also Chicano and Latin American. At the border they call me *chilango* or *mexiquillo*; in Mexico City it's *pocho* or *norteño*; and in Europe it's *sudaca*. The Anglos call me "Hispanic" or "Latino," and the Germans have, on more than one occasion, confused me with Turks or Italians. I walk amid the rubble of the Tower of Babel of my American postmodernity.

The recapitulation of my personal and collective topography has become my cultural obsession since I arrived in the United States. I look for the traces of my generation, whose distance stretches not only from Mexico City to California, but also from the past to the future, from pre-Columbian America to high technology, and from Spanish to English, passing through "Spanglish."

As a result of this process I have become a cultural topographer, border-crosser, and hunter of myths. And it doesn't matter where I find myself, in Califas or Mexico City, in Barcelona or West

Berlin; I always have the sensation that I belong to the same species: the migrant tribe of fiery pupils.

My work, like that of many border artists, comes from two distinct traditions, and because of this has dual, or on occasion multiple, referential codes. One strain comes from Mexican popular culture, the Latin American literary "boom," and the Mexico City counterculture of the 1970s . . . the other comes directly from Fluxus (a late-1960s international art movement that explored alternative means of production and distribution), concrete poetry, conceptual art, and performance art. These two traditions converge in my border experience and they fuse together.

In my intellectual formation, Carlos Fuentes, Gabriel García Márquez, Oscar Chávez, Felipe Ehrenberg, José Agustín, and Augusto Boal were as important as William Burroughs, Michel Foucault, Rainer Werner Fassbinder, Jacques Lacan, Vito Acconci, and Joseph Beuys.

My "artistic space" is the intersection where the new Mexican urban poetry and the colloquial Anglo poetry meet; the intermediate stage somewhere between Mexican street theatre and multimedia performance; the silence that snaps in between *corrido* and punk; the wall that divides "neográfica" (a 1970s Mexico City art movement involved in the production of low-budget book art and graphics) and graffiti; the highway that joins Mexico City and Los Angeles; and the mysterious thread of thought and action that puts Pan-Latin Americanism in touch with the Chicano movement, and both of these in touch with other international vanguards.

I am a child of crisis and cultural syncretism, half-hippie and half-punk. My generation grew up watching movies about *charros* (Mexican cowboys) and science fiction, listening to *cumbias* and tunes from the Moody Blues, constructing altars and filming in Super-8, reading *El Corno Em-plumado* and *Artforum*, traveling to Tepoztlán and San Francisco, creating and de-creating myths. We went to Cuba in search of political illumination, to Spain to visit the crazy grandmother, and to the United States in search of the instantaneous musico-sexual paradise. We found nothing. Our dreams wound up getting caught in the webs of the border.

Our generation belongs to the world's biggest floating population: the weary travelers, the dislocated, those of us who left because we didn't fit anymore, those of us who still haven't arrived because we don't know where to arrive at, or because we can't go back anymore.

Our deepest generational emotion is that of loss, which comes from our having left. Our loss is total and occurs at multiple levels: loss of our country (culture and national rituals) and our class (the "illustrious" middle class and upper-middle); progressive loss of language and literary culture in our native tongue (those of us who live in non-Spanish-speaking countries); loss of ideological meta-horizons (the repression against and division of the left) and of metaphysical certainty.

In exchange, what we won was a vision of a more experimental culture, that is to say, a multifocal and tolerant one.

Going beyond nationalism, we established cultural alliances with other places, and we won a true political conscience (declassicization and consequent politicization) as well as new options in social, sexual, spiritual, and aesthetic behavior.

Our artistic product presents hybrid realities and colliding visions within coalition. We practice the epistemology of multiplicity and a border semiotics. We share certain thematic interests, like the continual clash with cultural otherness, the crisis of identity, or, better said, access to trans- or multiculturalism, and the destruction of borders therefrom; the creation of alternative car-

DOCUMENTED/INDOCUMENTADO

tographies; a ferocious critique of the dominant culture of both countries; and, lastly, a proposal for new creative languages.

We witness the borderization of the world, by-product of the "deterritorialization" of vast human sectors. The borders either expand or are shot full of holes. Cultures and languages mutually invade one another. The South rises and melts, while the North descends dangerously with its economic and military pincers. The East moves west and vice versa. Europe and North America daily receive uncontainable migrations of human beings, a majority of whom are being displaced involuntarily. This phenomenon is the result of multiple factors: regional wars, unemployment, overpopulation, and especially the enormous disparity in North/South relations.

The demographic facts are staggering: the Middle East and Black Africa are already in Eu-

rope, and Latin America's heart now beats in the United States. New York and Paris increasingly resemble Mexico City and São Paolo. Cities like Tijuana and Los Angeles, once socio-urban aberrations, are becoming models of a new hybrid culture, full of uncertainty and vitality. And border youth—the fearsome "cholo-punks," children of the chasm that is opening between the "First" and the "Third" worlds, become the indisputable heirs to a new *mestizaje* (the fusion of the Amerindian and European races).

In this context, concepts like "high culture," "ethnic purity," "cultural identity," "beauty," and "fine arts" are absurdities and anachronisms. Like it or not, we are attending the funeral of modernity and the birth of a new culture.

In 1987, the unigeneric and monocultural vision of the world is insufficient. Syncretism, interdisciplinarianism, and multi-ethnicity are sine qua nons of contemporary art. And the artist or intellectual who doesn't comprehend this will be banished and his or her work will not form part of the great cultural debates of the continent.

Art is conceptual territory where everything is possible, and by the same token there do not exist certainties or limitations within it. In 1987, all the creative possibilities have been explored, and therefore they are all within our reach.

Thanks to the discoveries and advancements of many artists over the last fifteen years, the concept of métier is so wide and the parameters of art so flexible that they include practically every imaginable alternative: art as political negotiation (Felipe Ehrenberg—Mexico), as social reform (Joseph Beuys—Germany), as an instrument of multicultural organization (Judy Baca—United States) . . . or as alternative communication (Post Arte—Mexico, Kit Galloway and Sherri Rabinowitz—United States). Others conceive of art as a strategy of intervention aimed at mass media, or as citizen-diplomacy, social chronicle, a popular semiotics, or personal anthropology.

In 1987, our artistic options in terms of the medium, methodology, system of communication, and channels of distribution for our ideas and images are greater and more diverse than ever. Not understanding and practicing this freedom implies operating outside of history, or, worse yet, blindly accepting the restrictions imposed by cultural bureaucracies.

Our experience as Latino border artists and intellectuals in the United States fluctuates between legality and illegality, between partial citizenship and full. For the Anglo community we are simply "an ethnic minority," a subculture, that is to say, some kind of pre-industrial tribe with a good consumerist appetite. For the art world, we are practitioners of distant languages that, in the best of cases, are perceived as exotic.

In general, we are perceived through the folk-loric prisms of Hollywood, fad literature, and publicity; or through the ideological filters of mass media. For the average Anglo, we are nothing but "images," "symbols," "metaphors." We lack ontological existence and anthropological concreteness. We are perceived indiscriminately as magic creatures with shamanistic powers, happy bohemians with pretechnological sensibilities, or as romantic revolutionaries born in a Cuban poster from the 1970s. All this without mentioning the more ordinary myths, which link us with drugs, supersexuality, gratuitous violence, and terrorism; myths that serve to justify racism and disguise the fear of cultural otherness.

These mechanisms of mythification generate semantic interference and obstruct true intercultural dialogue. To make border art implies to reveal and subvert said mechanisms.

The term Hispanic, coined by techno-marketing experts and by the designers of political campaigns, homogenizes our cultural diversity (Chicanos, Cubans, and Puerto Ricans become indistinguishable), avoids our indigenous cultural heritage, and links us directly with Spain. Worse yet, it possesses connotations of upward mobility and political obedience.

The terms Third World culture, ethnic art, and minority art are openly ethnocentric and necessarily imply an axiological vision of the world at the service of Anglo-European culture. Confronted with them, one can't avoid asking the following questions: Besides possessing more money and arms, is the "First World" qualitatively better in any other way than our "underdeveloped" countries? Aren't the Anglos themselves also an "ethnic group," one of the most violent and antisocial tribes on this planet? Aren't the 500 million Latin American mestizos that inhabit the Americas a "minority"?

Among Chicanos, Mexicans, and Anglos, there is a heritage of relations poisoned by distrust and resentment. For this reason, my cultural work (especially in the camps of performance art, radio art, and journalism) has concentrated upon the destruction of the myths and the stereotypes that each group has invented to rationalize the other two.

With the dismantling of this mythology, I look, if not to create an instantaneous space for intercultural communication, at least to contribute to the creation of the groundwork and theoretical principles for a future dialogue that is capable of transcending the profound historical resentments that exist between the communities on either side of the border.

Within the framework of the false amnesty of the Immigration Reform and Control Act and the growing influence of the North American ultra-right, which seeks to close (militarize) the border because of supposed motives of "national security," the collaboration among Chicano, Mexican, and Anglo artists has become indispensable.

Anglo artists can contribute their technical ability, their comprehension of the new media of expression and information (video and audio), and their altruist/internationalist tendencies. In turn, Latinos (whether Mexican, Chicano, Caribbean, Central or South American) can contribute the originality of their cultural models, their spiritual strength, and their political understanding of the world.

Together, we can collaborate in surprising cultural projects without forgetting that both should retain control of the product, from the planning stages up through distribution. If this doesn't occur, then intercultural collaboration isn't authentic. We shouldn't confuse true collaboration with political paternalism, cultural vampirism, voyeurism, economic opportunism, and demogogic multiculturalism.

We should clear up this matter once and for all:

We (Latinos in the United States) don't want to be a mere ingredient of the melting pot. What we want is to participate actively in a humanistic, pluralistic, and politicized dialogue, continuous and not sporadic, and we want this to occur between equals who enjoy the same power of negotiation.

For this "intermediate space" to open, first there has to be a pact of mutual cultural understanding and acceptance, and it is precisely to this that the border artist can contribute. In this very delicate historical moment, Mexican artists and intellectuals as well as Chicanos and Anglos should try to "recontextualize" ourselves, that is to say, search for a "common cultural territory," and within it put into practice new models of communication and association.

Translated by Rubén Martínez

1989

THE BORDER IS . . .

(A MANIFESTO)

BORDER CULTURE IS A polysemantic term.

Stepping outside of one's culture is equivalent to walking outside of the law.

Border culture means boycott, complot, ilegalidad, clandestinidad, contrabando, transgresión, desobediencia binacional; en otros palabras, to smuggle dangerous poetry and utopian visions from one culture to another, desde allá, hasta acá.

But it also means to maintain one's dignity outside the law.

But it also means hybrid art forms for new contents-in-gestation: spray mural, techno-altar, poetry-in-tongues, audio graffiti, punkarachi, video corrido, anti-bolero, anti-todo: la migra (border patrol), art world, police, monocultura; en otras palabras y tierras, an art against the monolingües, tapados, nacionalistas, ex-teticistas en extinción, per omnia saecula speculorum . . .

But it also means to be fluid in English, Spanish, Spanglish, and Ingleñol, 'cause Spanglish is the language of border diplomacy.

But is also means transcultural friendship and collaboration among races, sexes, and generations.

But it also means to practice creative appropriation, expropriation, and subversion of dominant cultural forms.

But it also means a new cartography; a brand-new map to host the new project; the democratization of the East; the socialization of the West; the Third-Worldization of the North and the First-Worldization of the South.

But it also means a multiplicity of voices away from the center, different geo-cultural relations among more culturally akin regions: Tepito—San Diejuana, San Pancho—Nuyorrico, Miami—Quebec, San Antonio—Berlin, your home town and mine, digamos, a new internationalism ex centris.

But it also means regresar y volver a partir: to return and depart once again, 'cause border culture is a Sisyphean experience and to arrive is just an illusion.

But it also means a new terminology for new hybrid identities and métiers constantly metamorphosing: sudacá, not sudaca; Chicarrican, not Hispanic; mestizaje, not miscegenation; social thinker, not bohemian; accionista, not performer; intercultural, not postmodern.

But it also means to develop new models to interpret the world-in-crisis, the only world we know.

But it also means to push the borders of countries and languages or, better said, to find new

43

languages to express the fluctuating borders.

But it also means experimenting with the fringes between art and society, legalidad and illegality, English and español, male and female, North and South, self and other; and subverting these relationships.

But it also means to speak from the crevasse, desde acá, desde el medio. The border is the juncture, not the edge, and monoculturalism has been expelled to the margins.

But it also means glasnost, not government censorship, for censorship is the opposite of border culture.

But it also means to analyze critically all that lies on the current table of debates: multiculturalism, the Latino "boom," "ethnic art," controversial art, even border culture.

But it also means to question and transgress border culture. What today is powerful and necessary, tomorrow is arcane and ridiculous; what today is border culture, tomorrow is institutional art, not vice versa.

But it also means to escape the current co-optation of border culture.

But it also means to look at the past and the future at the same time. 1492 was the beginning of a genocidal era. 1992 will mark the beginning of a new era: America post-Colombina, Arteamérica sin fronteras. Soon, a new internationalism will have to gravitate around the spinal cord of this continent—not Europe, not just the North, not just white, not only you, compañero del otro lado de la frontera, el lenguaje y el océano.

THE MULTICULTURAL PARADIGM
AN OPEN LETTER
TO THE NATIONAL ARTS COMMUNITY

The following text was drafted after conversations with over thirty artists and cultural leaders from around the country. Quotes by colleagues are intertwined with my own views on the historical moment we are living as "Latinos" in the United States. Given the vertiginous speed with which contemporary culture metamorphoses, this document carries the risk of soon becoming outdated.

The quotes that appear without attribution are apocryphal statements found in the chaotic pages of my traveling notebooks. I don't remember who said them, yet I feel it is important to keep them as quotes to emphasize the paradigmatic and consensual nature of the document.

THE PARADIGM SHIFT

It's 1989 in this troubled continent accidentally called America. A major paradigm shift is taking place in front of our eyes. The East Coast/West Coast cultural axis is being replaced by a North/South one. The need for U.S. culture to come to terms with the Latino-American "cultural other" has become a national debate. Everywhere I go, I meet people seriously interested in our ideas and cultural models. The art, film, and literary worlds are finally looking South.

To look South means to remember; to recapture one's historical self. For the United States, this historical self extends from the early Native American cultures to the most recent immigration from Laos or Guatemala.

It's 1989 in this troubled country mistakenly called America. The current Latino and Asian immigration to the United States is the direct result of international conflicts between the so-called First and Third worlds. The colonized cultures are sliding into the space of the colonizer, and in doing so, they are redefining its borders and its culture. (A similar phenomenon is occurring in Europe with African immigration.)

The First and Third worlds have mutually penetrated one another. The two Americas are totally intertwined. The complex demographic, social, and linguistic processes that are transforming this country into a member of the "Second World" (or perhaps the "Fourth World"?) are being reflected in the art and thought produced by Latinos, African Americans, Asians, Native Americans, and Anglo-Europeans. Unlike the images on TV or in commercial cinema depicting a monocultural middle-class world existing outside of international crisis, contemporary U.S. society is fundamentally multiracial, multilingual, and socially polarized. So is its art.

Whenever and wherever two or more cultures meet—peacefully or violently—there is a border experience.

In order to describe the trans-, inter- and multicultural processes that are at the core of our contemporary border experience as Latino artists in the United States, we need to find a new terminology, a new iconography, and a new set of categories and definitions. We need to re-baptize the world in our own terms. The language of postmodernism is ethnocentric and insufficient. And so is the existing language of cultural institutions and funding agencies. Terms like Hispanic, Latino, ethnic, minority, marginal, alternative, and Third World, among others, are inaccurate and loaded with ideological implications. They create false categories and neo-colonial hierarchies. In the absence of a more enlightened terminology, we have no choice but to utilize them with extreme care.

My artistic sensibility as a deterritorialized Mexican/American artist living a permanent border experience cannot be explained solely by accepted historical notions of the twentieth-century Western vanguard (from dada to techno-performance). I am as Western and American as Laurie Anderson or Terry Allen. Yet my primary traditions are Chicano and Latin American art, literature, and political thought. We must realize that the West has been redefined. The South and the East are already in the West. And being American today means participating in the drafting of a new cultural topography.

Let's get it straight: America is a continent, not a country. Latin America encompasses more than half of America. Quechuas, Mixtecos, Yaquis, and Iroquois are American (not U.S. citizens). Chicano, Nuyorrican, Cajun, Afro-Caribbean, and Quebequois cultures are American as well. Mexicans and Canadians are also North Americans. Newly arrived Vietnamese and Laotians will soon become Americans. U.S. Anglo-European culture is but a mere component of a much larger cultural complex in constant metamorphosis.

This pluralistic America within the United States can be found, among other places, in the "Indian reservations" and the Chicano barrios of the Southwest, the African American neighborhoods of Washington, Chicago, or Detroit, or the multiracial neighborhoods of Manhattan, San Francisco, Los Angeles, or Miami. This sui generis America is no longer part of the First World. It still has no name or configuration, but as artists and cultural leaders, we have the responsibility to reflect it.

Despite the great cultural mirage sponsored by the people in power, everywhere we look we find pluralism, crisis, and non-synchronicity. The so-called dominant culture is no longer dominant. Dominant culture is a meta-reality that only exists in the virtual space of the mainstream media and in the ideologically and aesthetically controlled spaces of the monocultural institutions.

Today, if there is a dominant culture, it is border culture. And those who still haven't crossed a border will do it very soon. All Americans (from the vast continent America) were, are, or will be border-crossers. "All Mexicans," says Tomas Ybarra-Frausto, a Chicano theoretician in New York, "are potential Chicanos." As you read this text, you are crossing a border yourself.

INTERCULTURAL DIALOGUE

The social and ethnic fabric of the United States is filled with interstitial wounds, invisible to those who didn't experience the historical events that generated them, or who are victimized by historical amnesia. Those who cannot see these wounds feel frustrated by the hardships of intercultural dialogue. Intercultural dialogue unleashes the demons of history.

Arlene Raven, an artist and writer in New York, once told me, "In order to heal the wound, we first have to open it." In 1989, we are just opening the wound. To truly communicate with the cultural other is an extremely painful and scary experience. It is like getting lost in a forest of misconceptions or walking on mined territory.

The territory of intercultural dialogue is abrupt and labyrinthine. It is filled with geysers and cracks; with intolerant ghosts and invisible walls. Anglo-Americans are filled with stereotypical notions about Latinos and Latino-American art. Latin Americans are exaggeratedly distrustful of initiatives toward binational dialogue coming from this side/el otro lado. Bicultural Latinos in the United States (be they Chicanos, Nuyorricans, or others) and monocultural citizens of Latin America have a hard time getting along. This conflict represents one of the most painful border wounds, a wound in the middle of a family, a bitter split between two lovers from the same hometown.

Fear is the sign of the times. The 1980s are the culture of fear. Everywhere I go, I meet Anglo-Americans immersed in fear. They are scared of us, the other, taking over their country, their jobs, their neighborhoods, their universities, their art world. To "them," "we" are a whole package that includes an indistinct Spanish language, weird art, a sexual threat, gang activity, drugs, and "illegal aliens." They don't realize that their fear has been implanted as a form of political control; that this fear is the very source of the endemic violence that has been affecting this society since its foundation.

Border culture can help dismantle the mechanisms of fear. Border culture can guide us back to common ground and improve our negotiating skills. Border culture is a process of negotiation towards utopia, but in this case, utopia means peaceful coexistence and fruitful cooperation. The border is all we share/La frontera es lo único que compartimos.

My border colleagues and I are involved in a tripartite debate around separatism. Some Chicano nationalists who still haven't understood that Chicano culture has been redefined by the recent Caribbean and Central American immigrations feel threatened by the perspective of intercultural dialogue and Pan-Americanism. Meanwhile, sectors of the Mexican intelligentsia, viewing themselves as "guardians of Mexican sovereignty," see in our proposals for binational dialogue "a disguised form of integration" and pull back. Ironically, the conservative Anglo-Americans who are witnessing with panic the irreversible borderization of the United States tend to agree with Chicano and Mexican separatists who claim to speak from the left. The three parties prefer to defend "their" identity and culture, rather than to dialogue with the cultural other. The three parties would like to see the border closed. Their intransigent views are based on the modernist premise that identity and culture are closed systems, and that the less these systems change, the more "authentic" they are.

In 1989, we must realize that all cultures and identities are open systems in constant process of transformation, redefinition, and recontextualization. What we need is dialogue, not protection. In fact, the only way to regenerate identity and culture is through ongoing dialogue with the other.

Then, the question is, what does dialogue mean? Some thoughts in this respect:

Dialogue is a two-way, ongoing communication between peoples and communities that enjoy equal negotiating powers.

Dialogue is a micro-universal expression of international cooperation. When it is effective, we recognize ourselves in the other and realize we don't have to fear.

Dialogue has never existed between the First and Third worlds. We must not confuse dialogue with neo-colonialism, paternalism, vampirism, or appropriation.

Dialogue is the opposite of national security, neighborhood watch, racial paranoia, aesthetic protectionism, sentimental nationalism, ethnocentrism, and monolinguality.

In order to dialogue, we must learn each other's language, history, art, literature, and political ideas. We must travel south and east, with frequency and humility, not as cultural tourists but as civilian ambassadors.

Only through dialogue can we develop models of coexistence and cooperation. Only through an ongoing public dialogue in the form of publications, conferences, and collaborative intercultural art and media projects can the wound effectively heal. It will be a long process. It might take thirty to fifty years. We cannot undo centuries of cultural indifference, domination, and racism overnight. All we can aspire to is to begin a dialogue. This document is a humble contribution. I ask you to join in.

A whole generation of artists and intellectuals has begun the dialogue. It is mostly artists, writers, and arts administrators (not politicians, scientists, or religious leaders) who are leading this effort, and, of these people, the most vocal and enlightened are women. In the late 1980s, the true cultural leaders of our communities are women.

THE OTHER VANGUARD

U.S. Latino culture is not homogeneous. It includes a multiplicity of artistic and intellectual expressions both rural and urban, traditional and experimental, marginal and dominant. These expressions differ, depending on their creator's class, sex, nationality, ideology, geography, political context, degree of marginality or assimilation, and time spent in the United States.

California Chicanos and Nuyorricans inhabit different cultural landscapes. Even within Chicano culture a poet living in a rural community in New Mexico has very little in common with an urban cholo-punk from L.A. Right-wing Cubanos from Miami are unconditional adversaries of leftist South American exiles. The cultural expressions of Central American and Mexican migrant workers differ drastically from those of the Latino intelligentsia in the universities, ad infinitum. Even this document that attempts to present multiple voices and concerns cannot possibly reflect all sectors of our communities. There is no such thing as "Latino art" or "Hispanic art." There are hundreds of types of Latino-American-derived art in the United States. Each is aesthetically, socially, and politically specific.

The United States suffers from a severe case of amnesia. In its obsessive quest to "construct the future," it tends to selectively forget or erase the past. Fortunately, the so-called disenfranchised groups who don't feel part of this national project have been meticulously documenting their histories. Latinos, African Americans, Asians, women, gays, experimental artists, and non-aligned intellectuals have used inventive languages to record the other history from a multicentric perspective.

"Our art functions both as collective memory and alternative chronicle," says the San Francisco-based Chicana artist and critic Amalia Mesa-Bains. In this sense, this other art, if nurtured, can become a powerful tool to recapture the desired historical self. The great paradox is that without this historical self, no meaningful future can ever be constructed.

Métier is being redefined. In Latin America, the artist has multiple roles. He/she is not just an image-maker or a marginal genius, but a social thinker/educator/counterjournalist/civilian diplomat/human-rights observer. His/her activities take place in the center of society and not in specialized corners.

So-called minority artists in the U.S. have also been forced to develop multidimensional roles. In the absence of enough institutions that respond to our needs, we have become a sui generis tribe of community organizers, media interventionists, and alternative chroniclers. And the images, texts, and performances we produce are an integral part of these extra-artistic activities.

These models are much more pertinent to our times than those of the established art world.

Unlike the avant-garde of modernist times, today's avant-garde has multiple fronts, or, as Steven Durland has stated: "The avant-garde is no longer in the front but in the margins." To be avant-garde in the late 1980s means to contribute to the decentralization of art. To be avant-garde means to be able to cross the border; to go back and forth between art and politically significant territory, be it inter-racial relations, immigration, ecology, homelessness, AIDS, or violence toward women, disenfranchised communities, and Third World countries. To be avant-garde means to

perform and exhibit in both artistic and non-artistic contexts: to operate in the world, not just the art world.

In order to articulate our present crisis as cross-cultural artists, we need to invent and reinvent languages constantly. These languages have to be as syncretic, diverse, and complex as the fractured realities we are trying to define.

Postmodernism is a crumbled conceptual architecture, and we are tired of walking among someone else's ruins.

Border artists use experimental techniques and performance-derived practices to intervene directly in the world. The permanent condition of political emergency and cultural vulnerability we live in leaves us no other choice. If our actions are not daring, inventive, and unexpected, they won't make a difference, and border reality, with its overwhelming dynamics, will supercede us in an instant.

In this sense, the experimental nature of border art is informed more by political and cultural strategies than by postmodernist theory.

Like artists operating in other politically sensitive parts of the world, border artists understand that formal experimentation is only worthwhile in relation to more important tasks such as the need to generate a binational dialogue, the need to create cultural spaces for others, and the need to redefine the asymmetrical relations between the North and the South and among the various ethnic groups that converge in the border spiral. Confronted with these priorities, the hyperspecialized concerns of the art world appear to be secondary.

Much of the contemporary work produced by the Latino community is often regarded as anachronistic and traditional by the art world. Why?

Innovation for innovation's sake, New York's art obsession, doesn't really make sense to us. Innovation is not a value per se in our culture. What we consider "original" generally deals with extra-artistic concerns or concerns related to our traditions and the historical moment we live in. Because of this, our art never seems experimental enough to a monocultural observer.

The misunderstanding increases when the art world discovers that most of us aren't that interested in the gratuitous use of high technology or in the creation of special effects as an end in itself. Our rejection of unnecessary technology is seen as gratuitous technophobia rather than a political stance.

There are, in fact, many Latino artists working in computer art, media art, video, audio, and sophisticated multimedia languages, but they utilize technology in a socially responsible manner to reveal the contradictions of living and working between a pre-industrial past of mythical dimensions (the homeland) and a post-industrial present in permanent states of crisis.

When validating contemporary Latino artistic expressions (and this can also apply to African American, Asian American, and Native American art), critics must take off the ethnocentric glasses of innovation and approach the work within its own framework. To understand this framework, they have to do their homework.

Artistic quality is also relative. Hegemonic centers like New York, Paris, and Mexico City have manufactured sacred canons of universality and excellence that we are expected to follow in order to break out of regionalism or ethnicity. But these dogmas are crumbling. The cultural process that the United States is presently undergoing implies a shift of center, a decentralization of aesthetic canons and styles, and therefore a multiplication of validating criteria.

In 1989, we must always use multiple repertoires to analyze and appreciate a work of art or literature, especially if it comes from a non-Anglo-European source. Cultural multiplicity and aesthetic relativism must be familiar notions to contemporary curators, critics, journalists, arts organizers, panelists, and funding agents.

THE LATINO BOOM

What exactly is the "Latino Boom"?
The artists answer (choose one of the following):
   a) a kind of smoke screen to hide reality
   b) a prestidigitation act to distract us from politics
   c) the green light for us to become rich and famous
   d) a major opportunity to infiltrate and speak from within
   e) a contemporary version of the "good neighbor" policy toward Latin America
   f) the logical result of the Chicano and Nuyorrican movements
   g) the caprice of a Madison Avenue tycoon
(Choose one of the above answers and mail it to the education department of your local museum.)

In 1987, just like in 1492, we were "discovered" (re-discovered to be precise). We have been here for over 2,000 years; yet, according to *Time* magazine and many other publications, we "just broke out of the barrio." Today Latinos are being portrayed as the new "up and coming" urban sofisticados. We are suddenly in, fashionable, and grantable, and our ethnicity is being commodified. Why?

According to theorist Gayatry Spivak, "otherness has replaced postmodernism as the object of desire." We are undetermined "objects of desire" within a meta-landscape of Mac Fajitas, La Bamba crazes, MTV border rock, Pepsi ads in Spanish, and Chicano art without thorns.

In the same way that the U.S. government needs and wants a cheap, undocumented labor force to sustain its agricultural complex without having to suffer the Spanish language or unemployed foreigners wandering in their neighborhoods, the contemporary art world needs and desires the spiritual and aesthetic models of Latino culture without having to experience our political outrage and cultural contradictions. What the art world wants is a "domesticated Latino" who can provide enlightenment without irritation, entertainment without confrontation.

"They don't want the real thing. They want microwave tamales and Frida Kahlo T-shirts." They want ranchero music sung by Linda Ronstadt, not Lola Beltrán (the "queen" of Mexican ranchero music), the Mexicorama look of *The Milagro Beanfield War* and not the acidity of Chicano experimental video.

We must politely remind the art world that hype is never a substitute for culture. It is reality that must be addressed, no matter how painful or complex it might be. Like the border graffiti says: "Simulacra stops here" (at the border).

In this Faustian moment of perplexity and sudden attention given to "Latinos" by major cultural institutions and mainstream media, we are concerned about the way "Latino art" is being presented and re-presented.

Some frequent mistakes include homogenization (all Latinos are alike and interchangeable), decontextualization (Latino art is defined as a self-contained system that exists outside Western culture), curatorial eclecticism (all styles and art forms can be showcased in the same event as long as they are Latino), folklorization and exoticization (needless to explain) . . .

Latino artists are being portrayed as "magical realists," "pre-technological bohemians," "primeval creatures in touch with ritual," "hypersexual entertainers," "fiery revolutionaries," or "amazing success stories." Our art is being described as "colorful," "passionate," "mysterious," "exuberant," "baroque," etc., all euphemistic terms for irrationalism and primitivism.

These mythical views only help to perpetuate the colonizing notions of the South as a wild and exotic pre-industrial universe ever waiting to be discovered, enjoyed, and purchased by the entrepreneurial eye of the North.

It is mainly the artists who voluntarily or unknowingly resemble the stereotypes who end up being selected by the fingers of the Latino boom, but where are the voices of dissent who delineate the boundaries of the abyss? Where are the artists experimenting with the new possibilities of identity? Where are the artists working in performance, video, or installation, the more politicized ones? And where are the Latinas? Women have been instrumental in the creation of a Latino culture in the United States. Why are all these key artists being left out of the blockbuster Hispanic shows and the all-encompassing Latino festivals?

Some people think that these questions are an expression of our permanent dissatisfaction and ungratefulness. My response to them is simple. By asking out loud, we are merely trying to clean the mirror of true communication.

Many of us are ambivalent about the effects of the boom. On one hand, it has opened doors to many talented artists whose work was practically unknown outside the Latino milieu. On the other, it has brought foreign values to our milieu. Those chosen are pressured to become more slick and "professional" and therefore more individualistic and competitive, and to produce twice as much as before. The result is devastating: museum-quality art framed by cultural guilt and spiritual exhaustion. And on top of that, it has produced a confused community, divided into those who were chosen and those who weren't. Those left behind are slowly poisoned by jealousy and defeat.

Many of us don't aspire to make it in Hollywood or New York. We want something more ambitious. And that is to be in control of our political destiny and our cultural expressions. What the boom has done is to provide us with a handful of opportunities to "make it" at a very high spiritual cost. But it has not contributed to the betterment of the conditions of our communities.

There is a fatal discrepancy between the colorful image of prosperity broadcast by the boom and the sordid reality that no one wishes to address. Today, Latinos have the highest school drop-out rate. We are the largest population in the prisons of the Southwest. The majority of babies born with AIDS are Latino and African American. Police brutality, alcoholism, and drugs are quotidian realities in our communities. Even our physical space is being threatened. Gentrification is pushing our families and friends outside our barrios as we witness with melancholy and impotence the arrival of real-estate lords, insensitive yuppies, trendy restaurants, and commercial galleries. So, what exactly is booming?

The Latino boom is clearly a media-produced mirage, a marketing strategy designed with two objectives: to expand our consumer power and to offer new exotica to the American middle class. Our participation in national political and cultural processes remains restricted to token individuals who are generally conservative.

We want understanding, not publicity. We want to be considered intellectuals, not entertainers; partners, not clients; collaborators, not competitors; holders of a strong spiritual vision, not emerging voices; and, above all, full citizens, not exotic minorities.

THE MULTICULTURAL CRAZE OR "WE ARE THE (ART) WORLD" PART II
"2 Latinos + 2 Asians + 2 Blacks = Multicultural"
(conceptual T-shirt)

A multicultural fever of epidemic proportions is afflicting the art world. Everywhere we look, there are cultural institutions organizing events that feature artists from various ethnic communities that have almost nothing in common aesthetically or ideologically. "The only thing that binds us is otherness," says Amalia Mesa-Bains, "a threatening otherness that must be rationalized and made accessible."

"Multicultural" is the hip word of the late 1980s. Everybody agrees it is politically correct. Few know what it really means.

It is an ambiguous term. It can mean a cultural pluralism in which the various ethnic groups collaborate and dialogue with one another without having to sacrifice their particular identities to the Big Blob. But it can also mean a kind of Esperantic Disney World, a tutti-frutti cocktail of cultures, languages, and art forms in which "everything becomes everything else," and nothing is really indispensable. This is a dangerous notion that strongly resembles the bankrupt concept of the melting pot with its familiar connotations of integration, homogenization, and neutralization. It is why so many Latino organizations are so distrustful of the term.

Many key questions are still unresolved: Can "minority" groups or organizations who only produce work relevant to their milieu be considered multicultural? Given that Chicano culture is a culture of fusion between Mexican and Anglo-American, can we say that all Chicano spaces are by definition multicultural? Are Anglo-American women and gay groups part of this project? Can a group formed by a majority of Anglo-Americans, say eight out of ten, be considered multicultural? What is the difference between fusion, hybridization, synthesis, and appropriation? What is the difference between cross-, inter-, and multicultural?

The debate is open and we should all participate in sharpening the meaning of the word.

During the past twenty years, a number of pioneering non-white artists, writers, and institutions have been quietly but tenaciously paving the way toward the present multicultural craze. Yet they aren't getting recognition or funding. Some are even giving up for lack of support. Meanwhile, monocultural organizations with absolutely no track record of multicultural involvement have adopted the rhetoric of multiculturalism as a strategy to obtain substantial program funding. They often use this funding to commission Anglo artists who work with appropriated imagery.

What should be done? If a monocultural organization wants to apply for funding to produce "multicultural work" (and no one is questioning their right to do it), they must at least have the dignity to contact the various ethnic communities around them, ask for assistance, invite them to collaborate, and, if possible, hire people of color for permanent staff positions. To hire bilingual clerical staff and multiculturally literate archivists could be extremely helpful.

A provocative model is being implemented based on the temporary relationship between an alternative space and a local community organization with the common goals of sharing audiences and producing a specific event, an exhibit, or a publication. Other models must be brought forward.

Am I asking too much? Multiculturalism must be reflected not only in the programs or publicity of an organization, but in its administrative structure, in the quality of thought of its members, and eventually in the audience it serves.

I'm becoming exhausted repeating it: multiculturalism is not an art trend, not a grant language, nor a new investment package for art maquiladoras. It is the very core of the new society in which we live!

PARADOXES AND PROPOSALS

We are living a paradoxical moment. At the peak of the Latino boom and the multicultural craze, we witness with utter perplexity the most arrogant behavior of the current administration perpetrated against "minorities," immigrants, and Latin American countries.

In the very moment Eddie Olmos, Luis Valdez, Rubén Blades, and Los Lobos are becoming national celebrities, the U.S. government is threatening to dismantle bilingual education and affirmative action, and proposing to build a ditch on the U.S./Mexico border.

Just as my colleagues and I are being asked to perform and exhibit in the main spaces of Manhattan and San Francisco, the border patrol is dismantling labor camps in North County (San Diego) and the police in California are declaring open warfare against "Latino gangs."

On the same TV channels that show us glamorous commercials for Taco Bell, Colombian coffee, or Mexican beer, we also witness sensationalist accounts of Mexican criminals, drug dealers, and corrupt politicos on the evening news. The current media war against the Latino cultural other is intercut with eulogies to our products. Blood and salsa, that's the nature of this relationship.

It's all very confusing, but we are determined to find the underlying connections between these facts. For these connections can reveal important information about the way contemporary U.S. culture deals with otherness. In this context, my colleagues and I encourage our fellow artists, writers, journalists, curators, and cultural organizers to participate in this continental project, to collaborate (truly collaborate) as much as possible with the cultural other, inside and outside our borders, and to learn to share decisions and power with people of non-Anglo-European descent. Only through a continuous and systematic rejection of racism, sexism, and separatism can we come to terms with the otherness outside and the otherness within. From within, we must help the United States become an enlightened neighbor on this continent and a respectful landlord in its own house.

FROM ART-MAGEDDON TO GRINGOSTROIKA

A MANIFESTO AGAINST CENSORSHIP

TRACK I

FINISECULARTE [*Soundbed of Gregorian chants*]

WE APPROACH THE FINAL DECADE of the twentieth century with great perplexity. Unprecedented changes in the world have taken place in the past three years: from Tiananmen Square to the Persian Gulf and from Berlin to Panama City, we all felt the overwhelming birth pains of the new millennium. Unnecessary massacres, civil wars, ecological disasters, epidemics, and abrupt transformations of political regimes and economic structures shook both the planet and our individual psyches.

Major borders disappeared and others were instantly created. The communists finally crossed the Iron Curtain to go shopping, while the capitalists searched for nostalgia as tourists in the Eastern bloc. We felt like uninvited actors in a cyber-punk epic. The amount, complexity, and intensity of the changes made it impossible for us to decodify them adequately. Just as it had been in the Europe of the late 1400s, everything seemed to be up for grabs: ideology, identity, religious faith, language, and aesthetics. And in the middle of this *fin-de-siècle* earthquake, my contemporaries and I have been looking for a new

place to speak from, and a new vocabulary to describe this bizarre terra ignota we inherited.

The house of postmodernity is in ruins. We are citizens in a new society no longer defined by geo-politics, culture, or ideology, but by time. The clock of the decade is running. As members of the end-of-the-century society, the world in danger is our true and only neighborhood.

We are living inexplicable contradictions that shatter our understanding of the world: as the Soviet Union and Eastern Europe welcome structural changes, the U.S. power structure withdraws into its old republican model. As Latin America finally gets rid of its last military dictators, the United States becomes more heavily militarized. While diplomatic negotiation and intercultural dialogue emerge as viable options to construct a peaceful future (haven't we seen enough examples of transition-without-rupture in other countries?), the United Nations begins to practice panic politics in the Middle East. While other societies are being led by utopian reformists such as Mandela, Aristide, Havel, and Gorbachev, we are being misled by hemispheric machos.

While artists and writers in other countries are leading the way to the next century, we are being cut back, censored, and excluded from the political process. We face a strange historical dilemma: we stand equidistant from utopia and Armageddon, with one foot on each side of the border, and our art and thought reflect this condition.

TRACK II
THE CHILDREN OF THE FIRST AND THIRD WORLDS

[*Soundbed of punk-arachi music*]

In the 1980s, an increased awareness of the existence and importance of multicentric perspectives and hybrid cultures within the United States made us rethink the implications of "otherness." As a result of demographic shifts, generalized social turmoil, global media, and the exposure to non-Anglo-European art and thought—leading to intensified traffic between North and South and East and West—ethnocentric notions of "postmodernism" and "Western culture" were toppled by their own weight.

Latin America and Asia are already entrenched in North America; Africa slowly moves north into Europe; and, after a four-decade-long ideological divorce, Eastern and Western Europe are intermingling again.

The "West" is no longer West, and the "Third World" is no longer confined to the South. Old binary models, legacies of European colonialism and the Cold War mentality, have been replaced by a border dialectic of ongoing flux. We now inhabit a socio-cultural universe in constant motion, a moving cartography with a floating culture and a fluctuating sense of self. As artists, we now understand that we can speak two or more languages, have two or more identities and/or nationalities, perform different roles in multiple contexts, and not necessarily be in conflict with ourselves and others. Contradiction is no longer penalized. Hyphenated, transitional, and multiple identities are no longer just theories of radical anthropologists, but familiar pop-cultural realities. Furthermore, the "hybrids" of this and other continents (whether mulattos, mestizos, Chicanos, Nuyorricans, French Algerians, German Turks, British Pakistanis, or other more eccentric children of the First and Third worlds), are sliding toward the center of society. In doing so, they are rearranging the parameters of culture. The border experience is becoming "central," and the art and literature produced in the past five years can testify to this.

In this moving cartography, it becomes increasingly difficult to sustain separatist or essentialist positions. Multilingualism, syncretic aesthetics, border thought, and cultural pluralism are becoming common practices in the artistic and intellectual milieus of this continent, not because of matters of fashion as the dominant art world wishes to think, but because of a basic political necessity. To study the history, art, and political thought of our neighboring others and to learn Spanish and other languages becomes indispensable if we want to cross borders, regain our lost "American" citizenship, and participate in the drafting of the next century's cartography.

The holders of political, economic, and cultural power—including the broadcasting systems who shape and define our notions of the world—act extremely scared of these changes. Unable to comprehend their new place and role in this still incomprehensible cartography, they feel that the world and the future are no longer theirs, and they anxiously want them back. Their fears have reached neurotic proportions and their responses have been far from enlightened. They are currently doing everything they can to control the entry of the other, and to reconquer the not-so-New World, a territory that they feel by historical and cultural right belongs only to them.

TRACK III
LA MULTI-CONFUSIÓN
CULTI-MULTURAL

[*Soundbed by the Gypsy Kings or Mano Negra at the wrong speed*]

In many ways multiculturalism soured. We managed to turn the continent upside down so to speak, and insert the discourse, the terminology, and the attention toward non-Anglo-European experimental artists on the central platform of discussion. We even managed to alter the funding trends a bit. But we were unable to reform the administrative structure of the art institutions. They remain largely monocultural.

Today, many talk of how "exciting," "necessary," "confusing," or "exclusionary" "multiculturalism" is. Responses range from total willingness to fund and promote this cause, to militant anger at the prospect of sharing money and notoriety with artists from other ethnic backgrounds, to fighting about whose suffering deserves more attention.

The debate has already reached the mainstream, yet crucial political issues are still being avoided. Blockbuster exhibits present multicultural art as the "cutting edge"; yet, with a few exceptions, there is no mention of the historical crimes and social inequities that lie beneath the neocolonial relationship between Anglo-European culture and its surrounding others. Like the United Colors of Benetton ads, a utopian discourse of sameness helps to erase all unpleasant stories. The message becomes a refried colonial idea: if we merely hold hands and dance the mambo together, we can effectively abolish ideology, sexual and cultural politics, and class differences. Let's face it, the missing text is very sad: in 1991 racism, sexism, xenophobia, and ethnocentrism are alive and well in the U.S.A., and the communities that more proportionately reflect the multicultural composition of society are the homeless, the prisoners, people with AIDS, and the soldiers who just returned from the Persian Gulf.

The word multicultural hasn't even been defined. Due to the lack of an accumulative memory that codifies public debate in America, it seems that every year we have to restart the discussion from zero, and therefore we still can't agree on a basic definition. What are the differences between the multi-, inter-, intra-, and cross-cultural? What exactly do we mean by cultural equity, diversity, and pluralism? What are the differences between coexistence, exchange, dialogue, collaboration, fusion, hybridization, appropriation, and creative expropriation? These terms are very different. Some overlap and others even have opposite meanings; however, we often use them indiscriminately. As philosophers, practitioners, or impresarios of multiculturalism, we must ask some key questions: Which of these forms of relationship between cultures are more symmetrical and desirable and which are more reactionary? Which are those that truly empower marginalized groups? Which are new names for old ideas and which are new realities in search of a better name? Where exactly do we stand?

Artists and writers of color are losing patience. They have repeatedly stated that it is time to begin talking about economic and labor realities. In 1991, we should no longer need to be re-evaluating paradigms, contexts, and canons. Five years of excellent books, articles, and catalogues are available for those who arrive late to the intellectual banquet. Today, multiculturalism must also be understood as a question of workplace. All cultural institutions that claim to profess it must hire people of color in important administrative, artistic, and technical positions. They must be willing to share the paycheck, the desk, and the decision-making process with the other, not just the excitement of the artwork.

The enigmatic unwillingness of some "minority" artists and organizations to participate in the debate is also a matter of economics. They know that if they blindly join in, the larger organizations which have more connections, "credibility," and better grant writers will intercept their funding, and function as multicultural meta-sponsors.

We must watch out. The debate hasn't even engendered significant change and there is already a backlash: many Anglo-Americans who have been unable to find a place at the multicultural dinner table are becoming increasingly more vocal against racial, sexual, and political difference. The far-right is lumping all politicized matters of "otherness" under the label of "political correctness," and branding it "the new intellectual tyranny."

After 500 years of systematic exclusion and indifference they don't want to give us a few more years of attention. If we don't act fast to restore clarity to the debate, we might soon lose the little territory gained so painfully in the past five years.

The impulse behind the clumsy multicultural debate is the collective realization of the need to readjust our anachronistic national institutions and policies to the new social, cultural, linguistic, and demographic realities of this country. What we all are clumsily trying to say is that we want to be part of a "multi"-participatory society that truly embraces us all, including the multiracial and multisexual communities, the "hybrids," the recent immigrants from the South and the East, the children and elderly people—our most vulnerable and beloved ones, the people with AIDS, and the homeless—whose only mistake is not being able to afford housing. This is not radical politics but elemental humanism. From rap music to performance art, and from neighborhood politics to the international forums, our contemporary culture is already reflecting this quest.

TRACK IV
PERFORMANCE POLITICS OR POLITICAL PERFORMANCE ART

[*Sounds of crowds fading in and out of Brazilian heavy metal*]

Joseph Beuys prophesied it in the 1970s: art will become politics and politics will become art. And so it happened in the second half of the 1980s. Amidst abrupt changes in the political cartography, a mysterious convergence of performance art and politics began to occur. Politicians and activists borrowed performance techniques, while performance artists began to mix experimental art with direct political action.

An outstanding example is Superbarrio, the self-proclaimed "social wrestler" and charismatic political activist who emerged out of the ruins of a Mexico City devastated by the 1985 earthquake. Utilizing the mask and attire of a traditional Mexican wrestler, he became the leader of the Asamblea de Barrios, a grassroots organization that helped to rebuild the working-class neighborhoods affected by the quake and lobbied successfully for expanded housing programs. Behind the mask of Superbarrio there are at least four different activists, each involved in a specialized task: media intervention, grassroots politics, political theory, and real wrestling.

Another Mexican performance activist is Fray Tormenta, a Catholic priest who ventured into professional wrestling in order to earn the necessary money to build orphanages and bring media attention to the plight of abandoned children. In church, he wears his wrestling mask to give mass; in the wrestling ring, he challenges his opponents wearing religious vestments.

In Peru, Alberto Fugimori, the son of Japanese immigrants with no political experience, managed to win the last presidential elections by utilizing performance and media art tactics. At certain strategic moments of his electoral campaign he appeared in public dressed as a samurai.

In these Latin American examples, the mythical personae created by politicians and social activists function as both pop-cultural allegories and sophisticated media strategies.

During this same time, on this side of the border, East Coast art collectives such as Group Material, Grand Fury, and the Guerrilla Girls used guerrilla theatre, installation, and media-art strategies to draw attention to the AIDS crisis and to the art world's racist and sexist practices. On the West Coast, groups like the Border Arts Workshop and the Los Angeles Poverty Department employed experimental art methodologies to intervene directly in the realms of immigration and homelessness.

In one way or another, most artists, thinkers, and arts organizers were affected by the activist spirit of art and the performative nature of politics during the late 1980s.

The system tried to develop its antidotes. In Mexico, the government responded to the popularity of Superbarrio by creating a performance rival: Superpueblo. In the Southwest, many corporations hyped the border as a maquiladora (assembly plant) heaven to seduce investors, and many mainstream cultural institutions followed suit. The pseudo-Mexican food chain Taco Bell began designing placemats inspired by the conceptual murals of border artists. Even the far-right began to appropriate the performance tactics of its opponents. In 1990, a large caravan of anti-Mexican "concerned citizens" and white supremacists started monthly gatherings at the San Diego-Tijuana border fence, with their car headlights pointing South as a protest against "the Mexican invasion." When questioned by artist Richard Lou, San Diego's former mayor Roger Hedgecock, who spearheaded the entire campaign, answered, "We are doing border art." Fortunately, the reaction of the Tijuanenses was

more original and poetic: in their counter-performances, they responded with mirrors and candles.

Track V
Censura No Es-Cultura
[Soundbed of porno-rap]

During these troubled years, art in the United States became a highly symbolic territory of retaliation. Ultra-conservative religious and government sectors began to target non-commercial art depicting sexual, racial, and ideological alternatives to patriarchal WASP culture. As in the McCarthy era, artists once again were confronted with the spectre of a blacklist, spaces were closed, and cultural organizers were sent to court. This time the strategy was to use sexual morality instead of ideology as a pretext to condemn works of art that confronted mythical American values. Not coincidentally, most of the artwork chosen as "controversial" was done by gay, women, African American, and Latino artists.

This time, censorship was part of a much larger political spectrum. Symptoms of a totalitarian state, the logical progression of a decade under the Reagan-Bush administration, were being felt everywhere. The over-reaction of Jesse Helms and the American Family Association to sexually explicit art, the attempts to dismantle affirmative action and bilingual education, the efforts to ban the basic right of women to control their own bodies, the silent militarization of the Mexican border, the government's unwillingness to respond to AIDS and homelessness, the euphemistic war on drugs, the illegal invasion of Panama, the display of military bravado in the Persian Gulf, and the presidential veto of the civil rights legislation were all different expressions of the same censoring mentality, and fear of otherness was at its core.

Since its foundation, the United States has used the strategy of attacking the cultural and ideological other to consolidate itself. From above, American identity has been defined in opposition to an evil other. From Native Americans to Soviets, this other had to first be demonized and dehumanized in order to then be justifiably caricatured, controlled, exploited, or destroyed.

With the end of the Cold War and the sudden disappearance of the communist threat, new enemies had to be invented. First on the list were Mexican migrant workers blamed for growing unemployment created by elitist government policies. Then came Colombian and Mexican drug-lords led by General Manuel Antonio Noriega, but their past association with the White House made them a bad choice. Then came African American and Latino "gangs" from the inner cities who were blamed for urban violence and for the drug problem of the American middle and upper class. Next on the list were Japanese businessmen who were "silently buying our country," and, later on, gay and "controversial" artists of color whose art reflected a society in crisis, a reflection that Washington didn't want to look at. Finally came the "monstrous" Iraqis, and by extension, all Arabs, Arab-looking people, and people who opposed the war.

All progressive and disadvantaged others who weren't born Christian, male, white, and wealthy seem to be, in one way or another, impeding the construction of the New World (dis)Order. This much-touted Order is a unique autocratic utopia based in one point of view—theirs. All others inside and outside the United States—whether experimental artists, non-aligned intellectuals, undomesticated African Americans and Latinos, women, gays, homeless people, or foreigners from unfriendly countries—have now begun to suffer in our own skin the repercussions of this sinister Order.

We are astonished and profoundly scared, for now we know that after the exoneration of Oliver North and the Baghdad genocide, the victorious politicos in Washington and their European side-kicks are capable of anything. The militant ethnocentrism of these new crusaders reminds us of the original Spanish and British colonizers of the American continent, who perceived cultural differences as signs of danger.

Despite our fear, we must never lose this perspective. Any artist, intellectual, or arts organizer who believes in and practices civil and human rights, cultural pluralism, and freedom of expression is voluntarily or involuntarily a member of a resistance against the forces that seek to take our basic rights away from us. And his/her words, images, and actions are expressions of the zeitgeist of America, the other America, the one to which we truly belong.

TRACK VI
...AND THEY ARRIVED
WITHOUT PAPERS

[*Soundbed of melancholic Tarahumara violins*]
Another important issue haunting our consciousness is the need to redefine the 500-year celebration of the alleged "discovery of America," a blatant euphemism for the genocide that made Latin America into a subsidiary of Europe, and America into the United States. Christopher Columbus introduced to the New World a model of cultural domination and racial extermination that has sadly survived into the present. Today, the discovery and conquest of America continue to be re-enacted on multiple stages throughout the continent in such places as the Amazon, Central America, the U.S./Mexico border, African American and Latino neighborhoods, and the Native American "reservations" of the United States.

499 years later the original inhabitants of this land are still lacking basic human rights, access to education, decent housing, and medical care. The

conquistadors have been replaced by slick politicos and corporate businessmen, and their mercenaries by mestizo soldiers, psychotic Marines, and racist border guards. Relocated to Washington, the New Inquisition is now indicting artists and gays, and enforcing English as the "Official Language" in the Southwest. Other cultures are still regarded as violent or simplistic by our dominant media institutions. "Undesirable foreigners," who paradoxically come from countries previously destabilized by the United States itself, continue to be deported just as the Jews and Arabs were expelled from Spain in 1492.

Regrettably the ghost of undocumented Columbus is still around. As the Native Americans say, "Columbus Day," which in Mexico is known as "El Día de la Raza," must be renamed "the day of indigenous dignity," and the fall of Tenochtitlan "the day of indigenous resistance." The euphemistic word "discovery" must be replaced by "invasion" or "intervention" (or at least by "culture shock"), and the term "quincentennial," which has a celebratory connotation, must be exchanged for the purely descriptive word "quincentennary." Inexact labels referring to ethnicity, such as "Hispanic," "White," "Black," and "Indian," should be replaced by the terms those groups determine for themselves.

The "discovery" marked the begining of a 500-year era in which Europeans and North Americans assumed the right to name everyone else, and this must end. We must not forget that before the Europeans arrived, there were more than 1,000 different cultures on this continent, each with a different name, and most, despite uninterrupted genocide, culturcide, and disease, are still alive. From Alaska to Patagonia, and from Quito to Quebec, non-aligned artists, writers, and activists are preparing for the great counter-celebration. Wherever we turn, there are people organizing conferences, exhibits, pilgrimages, and performance actions. The books, films, albums, and performances that will present the other chronicle are currently in the making. To participate in this continental project and to propose more enlightened models for the relationship between the Old and New worlds (and therefore between North and Latin America), is crucial to any group who doesn't wish to propagate the bloody European and North American legacy on this continent.

TRACK VII
RESPONSES TO PANIC CULTURE
[*Music by Jello Biafra and the Native American Bird Singers*]

My generation was born and raised in a world of multiple crises and continuous fragmentation. Our current lives are framed by the sinister Bermuda triangle of war, AIDS, and recession. We seem to be closer than ever to the end, and precisely because of this, our actions have twice as much meaning and moral weight, though perhaps fewer repercussions.

Our fragile contemporaries are starving, migrating, and dying at a very young age, and the art we are making already reflects this sense of emergency. But it is not enough to just make art. We must step outside of the safe art arena and attempt to recapture our stolen political will and mutilated civic self.

As the 1990s unfold, U.S. artists, cultural organizers, and intellectuals must perform central roles in the making of a society beyond Columbus. We must fine-tune our multiple roles as intercultural diplomats, border philosophers, chroniclers, and activists for world glasnost and local gringostroika. More than ever, we must practice, promote, and demand access, tolerance, dialogue, and reform.

We must speak with valor and clarity, from the new center, not the old margins, and we must do it in large-scale formats and for large and diverse audiences. We must use public access TV, National Public Radio, printed media, video, film, and fax art. We must take advantage of high technology. We must redefine and expand the activist legacy of the late 1980s to form more intercultural collectives, computer data banks, and publications linking various artistic, political, and media communities within and outside the country.

We must defend the survival of the art world as a demilitarized zone. We must continue to support the community centers and the alternative spaces which are potentially facing extinction. Large institutions must try to keep the smaller ones from sinking, for without them, the large institutions would lose their roots and their seeds. Successful painters might contemplate donating the proceeds from the sale of an artwork to a community center or an alternative space. In some cases, one painting or sculpture might be enough to pay for several months of operational expenses. If some of the smaller spaces cannot survive the crisis, we must develop different models that respond to the new conditions of cultural emergency.

We must listen carefully to other cultures who have a long history of facing repression, censorship, and exclusion. Native Americans, Latinos, African Americans, and Asian Americans have been fighting these battles for centuries.

We must rebuild community through our art, for our communities have been dismembered. The insidious colonial tendencies we have internalized—and that express themselves in sadistic competition for money and attention, political cannibalism, and moral distrust—must be overcome. We must realize that we are not each other's enemies and that the true enemy is currently enjoying our divisiveness.

We must dialogue and collaborate with artists from other disciplines and ethnic communities, as well as with political activists, educators, lawyers, journalists, cultural critics, and social scientists. The old schism between artists and academics must be resolved once and for all. We must come to the realization that we have been equally marginalized by society and that therefore we need one another. Artists need the intellectual rigor of academics and they need our skills to popularize issues. Academics have access to more extensive information and we have access to more diverse audiences. Together, we can develop a national consensus of priorities and strategies for the new decade.

Some people say that the 1990s will be "the decade of the environment," and I wish with all my heart they will be right, but, as performance artist Ellen Sebastian says, "We, the human beings, are the ultimate environment." From São Paolo to Baghdad, and from Soweto to the Bronx, we are a fauna in danger of extinction. Our eco-systems, the deteriorated multiracial cities we inhabit, are part of the nature we must save. If we don't save the human being and his/her concentrated habitat, we won't even be here to witness the extinction of the great whale and the California condor.

In times such as these, nationalism is no longer useful. The survival of the human species is a concern to all communities. As responsible artists of this end-of-the-century society, we must challenge the anachronistic notion that says we are only meant to work within our particular ethnic, political, or sexual communities, strictly art contexts, or marginal leftist milieus. Our place is the world-in-danger, as big as it can be for each of us, and our communities have multiplied exponentially. Regardless of age, race, gender, métier, or nationality, any socially responsible person—not just artists—from this or other continents who truly believes in and practices cultural democracy and racial and sexual equity must be considered a member of "our" community.

Parallel to this major project, a much more private and discrete, but equally important, path must be pursued: the humanization of our personal universe. We must learn to take good care of ourselves and our loved ones. If we are not responsible and loving friends, sons and daughters, parents, lovers, neighbors, and colleagues, how can we possibly be responsible citizens at large? If we don't recapture the necessary time and personal space to enjoy community rituals, friendship, food, exercise, and sex, where will we get the strength to continue?

The humanization of our disjointed lives is also an expression of the search for a new social order, and the reawakening of our total self—civilian, political, spiritual, erotic, and aesthetic—will inevitably demand a new social body to contain it.

TRACK VIII
THE CULTURE OF THE END OF THE CENTURY

[*Soundbed composed by the reader*]

I want to exercise my political imagination for a moment and try to imagine the place of the artist in a post-gringostroika society.

Perhaps in the 1990s, politicized artists and intellectuals in the United States will no longer be border pirates or alternative chroniclers, but respectable social thinkers. Perhaps a multiracial group of artists and arts organizers will head a Ministry of Cultural Affairs. Perhaps there will even be a Ministry of Cultural Affairs with a budget equivalent to that of other countries, and more than a hundred experimental artists will be able to survive exclusively from their art. Perhaps there will be a Free Art Agreement between the United States, Mexico, and Canada, and we will be able to exchange ideas and artistic products, not just consumer goods and hollow dreams.

Perhaps the Spanglish Only Initiative will replace English Only. Perhaps the border with Latin America, the Great Tortilla Curtain, will finally collapse. Perhaps one of these days Chicana artist Amalia Mesa-Bains will become governor of California, and performance artist Tim Miller or John Malpede the mayor of Los Angeles. Perhaps poet Victor Hernández Cruz will become president of Independent Puerto Rico and Noam Chomsky, U.S. Secretary of Information. Perhaps Ralph Nader will be Secretary of the Environment and Luis Valdez, the head of a generous INS. Perhaps performance artists will be heard regularly on National Public Radio, and poets and philosophers of color will publish daily in the major newspapers. Wouldn't you like to read the opinions of Cheri Moraga, James Luna, or Essex Hemphill in your local paper? Perhaps we will be able to watch Trinh T. Minh-Ha, Jessica Haggedorn, Gayatry Spivak, Michele Wallace, Coco Fusco, Gloria Anzaldua, Cornel West, Rubén Martínez, James Clifford, and many other thinkers from the other America on multilingual national television. Perhaps there will be at least five cultural TV channels in every city, and every independent film and video art piece will be available in the local video store. Perhaps we will be able to purchase books by Chicano, African American, Asian American, and Native American writers at the supermarket, even in 7-Eleven. Perhaps there will be so many alternative spaces that they will no longer be called alternative. Perhaps there will no longer be a need for community centers, since every city will function as a real community. Perhaps there will be so many artists and intellectuals of color working in our cultural, educational, and media institutions that there will no longer be a need to label us by our ethnicity. Perhaps we will no longer need to imagine.

PERFORMANCE

TEXTS

CALIFAS

por
GUILLERMO GÓMEZ-PEÑA
EL "MR. MISTERIO"

CALIFAS

Califas is a bilingual performance poem. The structure is disnarrative and modular, like the border experience. This makes it possible to recycle parts into other formats such as performance, radio-art, and video. There are two levels: the narrative, which describes "impossible situations" that subvert historical, political, and cultural facts; and the poetical level, which operates as memory or inner monologue. The poetical level is told by several mythic characters. *Califas* was commissioned by filmmakers Philip and Amy Brookman in 1987 for their film *My Other Self/Mi Otro Yo,* an experimental documentary on Chicano art in California. In this film, an epic poem replaces the traditional narrative voice. Fragments of *Califas* were used as part of "Border-X-Frontera," a radio-art piece created by Gómez-Peña and David Schein.

I. El Aztec Poet
in 1492, an Aztec sailor
named Noctli Europzin Tezpoca
departed from the port of Minatitlán
with a small flotilla of wooden rafts.
3 months later
he discovered a new continent
& named it Europzin after himself.
in November 1512,
the omnipotent Aztecs
began the conquest of *Europzin*
in the name of thy father Tezcatlipoca
lord of cross-cultural misconceptions
"I remember . . ."
—said the drunken Aztec poet—
"when our continent
still had no name
& we had no foreign tongues
to lick the things of the world
nicaya

the funky days
of my childhood are over
the crystal days
of my childhood were shattered
by their arrival."
"Spanish, French, Anglo-Saxon,
notecuiyohuan!"—he screamed
while holding a bottle of Sauza
as a wireless mike—
"who called you by the way?
Cortés, Maximilian, Ronald the First,
did anyone ask you to come?"

II
El Chicano Shaman
it's 1987
occéntlapal
& the sky is clotted with blood
the migras keep thinking
they're able to stop
the historical undercurrents
of a continent gone bananas
may Tata God, el que embotella,
bless their unlimited stupidity.
[*In chorus*]
"unlimited the rivers of Brazil
unlimited the passion of my jaina
unlimited the sadness of the beast
suburbia, suburbia, suburbia . . ."

"I remember . . ."
—said Chicano shaman-en-trance—
"when there was no South or North
but a continuous cardinal vertigo
& one could walk collaterally
toward any image or sound
but today
life is different, tlatoque,
the New York darlings
have monopolized
the right to perceive"

today es dark & foggy
& Reagan is coughing backstage."
Chicano shaman freezes
in the video screen
Chicano murals
are X-rays of his memory,
"no one was there to imagine
that this land of encounters
called Califas
would be mortally sliced in half
Chicanos & Mexicanos
nos otros & aquellos
los amputados
del
más allá
del what you say . . ."

III
El Young Campesino
the young campesino
carefully licked
the bicultural breasts
of a border madonna
before adventuring
into the Otay Triangle
& then he opened his wings
as a female voice
began to whisper over his memory—
"dejarás a tu jaina embarazada
cruzarás la frontera de rodillas
pasarás desapercibido
como el pólen
& un día
tristeando por la Broadway
empezarás a recordar
que lo negado
como la fruta fresca a la mordida
también te corresponde."

he left the country paraphrasing the falcon
& when the falcon was wounded in mid-air

he lost his right wing
& joined El Movimiento

10 years later he wrote:
"querido hermano de la memoria clandestina
I used to be Telpócatl
el mero mero
el 7 máscaras, you know
but one night
someone stole my liver
& I learned this other language

querido hermano de la resistencia estética
I purged my ethnic resentments
in the eerie cantinas
of San Fernando & San Joaquín
building roads for someone else's thoughts
but when El Movimiento began
we all began to remember
instead of being remembered."

IV
EL JOHNNY

I saw the ethno-police
busting a young Chicano
for breathing
El Johnny looked at him
through his granpa's glasses
& asked en Califeño—
"Nomás for cruisin' carnal?
si llevo 20 siglos caminando"
cruisin' low
from Aztlán to Tenochtitlán
& back
through Tijuas or Juárez
en camión de 3 estrellas
cuarrás into the barrio.
"Califas qué fais?
Tlatoani en rollerskates."
—asked the pinche pig—
"aquí nomás Califa Ruíz

Californiando
a to' color californico
where all realities join
to become meta-ficción . . ."

"que what I'm doin' carnal?
aquí nomás Satanás
sailing on rivers of Chevys & Mustangs
& while sailing
on someone else's perception
we shipwreckkkk . . .
la vida es el Gran Cruisin."
—El Johnny continues calógicamente
   rapeando—
"cruseando
low & tight
through the Big Smoke
low & tight
from Tijuas to La Logan
low & tight
from Santa Ana to Ventura
stoppin' in Pacoima
to cry for a vision
& eat some chili beans
cooked by a Texan evangelist
in drag, ay, ay
cruisin' low & tight
is better than waiting
for Armageddon
in a plexiglass condo . . .
cruisin' sin pecado
while looking for the axis
to write
to fight for the right
to remember
to reconstruct two cities
in the valley of our memory
right here
we are
ciudadanos de la partida
peregrinos de la chingada."

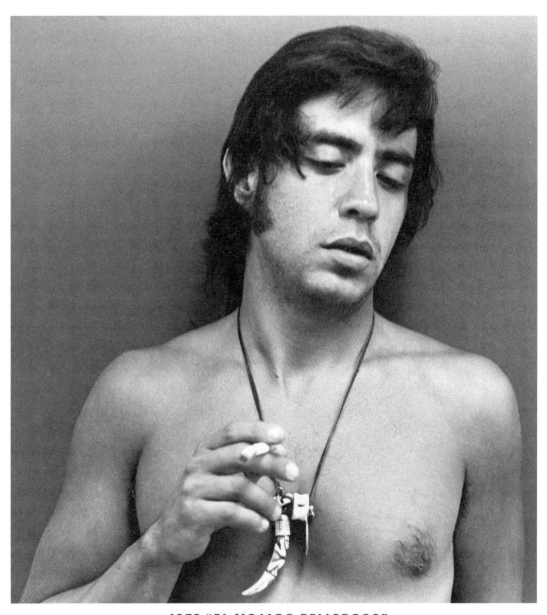

1979 "EL MOJADO PELIGROSO"

Staged photo of Gómez-Peña in a detention center of the INS. This was accompanied by a text. (From the archives of Poyesis Genética).

El Johnny & friends are busted by the ethno-
   police:
"nationality?"
"I'm from Sacra but
my parents were from Mérida
he's from San Fran
his parents were from Mochis
she's from East Los
her mother was from Puebla
& so on & so forth
it's confusing
we know
our nation extends
from the tip of Patagonia
to the peak of your
tortured imagination."

V

standing on the corner of Broadway & Hell
where English meets Spanish
& Death performs the last striptease of the day
El Johnny longs for his inner carnales
al Sueño lo torcieron
al Misterioso lo balacearon
& a Susy la Sad Girl
la trituraron los medios de información
"Mexico is sinking
California is on fire
& we all are getting burned
aren't we? we're just
a bunch of burning myths!"
—he begins to yell at the gringos—
"but what if suddenly
the continent turned upside down?
what if the U.S. was Mexico?
what if 200,000 Anglosaxicans
were to cross the border each month
to work as gardeners, waiters
musicians, movie extras
bouncers, babysitters, chauffeurs,
syndicated cartoons, featherweight

boxers, fruit-pickers & anonymous poets?
what if they were called waspanos,
waspitos, wasperos or waspbacks?
what if we were the top dogs?
what if literature was life?
what if yo were you
& tú fueras I, Mister?"

the Linguistic Patrol busted El Johnny again
for speaking too loud in an unknown tongue
at a cowboy cafe named La Esperanza
ay, the Linguistic Patrol forgives no one

he left the prison to become a poet
but instead
they sent him to Vietnam
& now they are sending his son
little Joe Superrealista
straight to Tegucigalpa
to teach his carnales

to kill their other carnales
little Joe will go to bed
with the Big Albino Mamma
of Continental Affairs
"hi, Joey, I'm la Big Jane,
the paramilitary queen, ajuua!
& you are here
to lick
my digital chakras."

VI
QUETZALCÓATL, JR.

today es dark & foggy
& Reagan is coughing backstage
tomorrow Quetzalcóatl will disembark
on the shores of La Jolla
to investigate the crimes of the local police
"dear citizens of California"
—he will say with a thick Mexican accent—
"your local police

is our continental nightmare."
flash forward:
Quetzalcóatl bursts into flames
in front of a hundred tourists
Tlatoani-bonzo ni martir
no traces
of ancient cultures in town
just the tire tracks
of an old Cadillac
& los chavales
chapoteando con la muerte
en los desérticos suburbios
de Aztlán ocupado.
even the telephone line is busy.

VII
EL MULTIMEDIA PACHUCO

East Los
nopalera de néon
a media noche
irrumpe el punk-mariachi
erupts like magma
entre pyramids de estuco
todo es ira y bancarrota
las patrullas rechinando
y la vírgen que estrena
sus medias de rayón
su brassier de concha nácar
while los chucos
tras the curtain
se emperifollan
2 puños y 15 flancos
to dance the night away

it's all fine & very cinematic
but what exactly am I doing here?
& who is shooting the pinche film?
Take Five:
"soy Tlapehuiani
el que ojea"

—Multimedia Pachuco
confesses to his street audience—
"& you'd better watch out
tlapecuihuixtli
ojo de computadora infectada
'cause ojo por ojo
is the law of my pen
my bilingual pen sketches
on your monolingual systems
remember
from Torquemada to Simpson-Rodino
we've been the wounded prey
but now, matador
we know our options."

"don't merely evoke the past"
—Gran Vato suggests
while lighting his Ganya taco—
"place yourself
in the lungs of the future
& from there
bien afilado
reinvent the entire continent
if necessary
turn it upside down
contra cultura no hay antídoto."

VIII
THE OAXACAN MAID

"there is a whisper within you
that reminds me
of who I am
néhuatl nimopo
néhuatl aic onimitzcócoli"
—thinks Elia, the Oaxacan maid
while rubbing a floor in Malibu.
she works for someone she'll never meet.
"néhuatl nimat"
—she whispers to her other self

la señora agoniza en la terraza
& los soldados conceptuales
patrullan el vecindario

"I remember the day
I disembarked
at a lonely Greyhound station
ay, the way *they* looked at me
Cortés & bunch looked at me
with more respect,
but respect nowadays
is a shredded gardenia."

"but who are *they*?"
—a wino inquires
"*them*, you know,"
—she replies—
"the enchilada-hunters
fumiga-latinos
shooting at their own fears
& their fears Tlatoani
overlap with our dreams."

"aaahhh, that's dangerous!" —he says—
"there are legal monsters roaming around."

"you got it Sauzaman
who are you by the way?"
—she asks the paleolithic wino
"a drunken Aztec poet
miento
Chicano shaman-en-trance
the young ex-campesino
Tlatoani en rollerskates
Multimedia Pachuco
Gran Vato Sauzaman
or better said
a bunch of broken myths
a bunch of fading images
a bunch of bad performances

my words are broken crystal
& you are meant to step on them."

IX

the Oaxacan maid
daydreams at the mirror—
"trazando caminos andamos
entre barrios & mentes
con los sucios pinceles de la memoria
aaahhh" —she sighs—
"my proletarian memory
my subemployed fingers
my pre-Columbian torso
my holy vagina, la panochtzin . . ."
—she faints into the mirror—
"aaaahhhhhhhh . . ."
there's nowhere else to go
the South has been destroyed
the North is occupied
by Reagan's conceptual battalion

semantic leaves across the border
semantic ravens across the fence
a hundred umbilical cords
hang from the barbed wire
& a naked performance artist
alias GGP
counts down with his toes
in Spanglish
10
9
8
7
6
5
4
3
2
"I see no rest for your soul
in the coming decade

no place for your ideas
in the world as it is"
—says Multimedia Pachuco from the mirror—
"he/she who paints or writes
articulating the maddening saga
of a continent without a name;
he/she without spinal cord or papers
must find a place to rest & wait
& when the eagle becomes a knife
& English has fully devoured our tongues
then, my dear jaina,
Afrodita con safos
Spanish will emerge from the ashes
like a gorgeous papagallo
& you & I will dance
a sweaty cumbia at the Palladium."

X
ALL INNER CHARACTERS IN CHORUS
"I see a whole generation
freefalling toward a borderless future
incredible mixtures beyond sci-fi
cholo-punks, pachuco krishnas
Irish concheros, high-tech mariachis
Indian rockers & Anglosandinistas
I see them all
wandering around
a continent without a name
the forgotten paisanos
howling corridos in Selma & Amarillo
the Mixteco pilgrims
heading North toward British Columbia
the Australian surfers

waiting for the B-wave at Valparaíso
the polyglot Pápagos
waiting for the sign to return
the Salvadoreans coming north to forget
the New Yorkers going south to remember
la T.J. whore
reciting Neruda from a taxi
the L.A. junkie
promoting the Contadora principles
Fuentes & Márquez
scolding the First World on MTV
Lacandonian shamans
exorcising multi-nationals at dawn
yuppie tribes paralysed by guilt & fear
all passing through Califas
en-transit to their other selves."

XI
THE AUTHOR
[*pre-recorded*]
standing on the map of my political desires
I toast to a borderless future
with our Alaskan hair
our Canadian head
our U.S. torso
our Mexican genitalia
our Central American cojones
our Caribbean sperm
our South American legs
our Patagonian feet
jumping borders at ease
amén, hey man.

1988-89

BORDER BRUJO

PROGRAM NOTES

BORDER BRUJO is a ritual, linguistic, and performative journey across the United States/México border.

BORDER BRUJO first crossed the border in costume in June of 1988.

BORDER BRUJO unfolds into fifteen different personae, each speaking a different border language. The relationship among these personae are symbolic of those between North and South, Anglo and Latin America, myth and social reality, legality and illegality, performance art and life. The structure is disnarrative and modular, like the border experience.

BORDER BRUJO speaks in Spanish to Mexicans, in Spanglish to Chicanos, in English to Anglo-Americans and in tongues to other brujos, locos, and border crossers. Only the perfectly bicultural can be in complicity with him.

BORDER BRUJO exorcises with the word the demons of the dominant cultures of both countries.

BORDER BRUJO articulates fear, desire, trauma, anger, and misplacement.

BORDER BRUJO suffers in his own flesh the pain of his fragmented community.

BORDER BRUJO puts a mirror between the two countries and then breaks it in front of the audience.

BORDER BRUJO loves and hates his audience, loves and hates himself.

Border Brujo creates a sacred space to reflect on the painful relationship between self and other. He dances between self and other. He becomes self and other, within himself.

Border Brujo is a performance character, but he is also an alternative chronicler of life in a community.

Border Brujo is a performance artist, but he is also a cultural prisoner, a migrant poet, a homeless shaman, and the village fool.

Border Brujo performs indiscriminately inside and outside the art world. He has appeared in galleries, museums, and theatre festivals, and also at youth centers, migrant-worker centers, high schools, community events, political rallies, and performance pilgrimages.

Border Brujo is another strategy to let YOU know we are here to stay, and we'd better begin developing a pact of mutual cultural understanding.

COSTUMES: altar jacket, pachuco hat, mariachi hat, wrestler masks, wig, dark glasses, banana necklace.

PROPS: portable altar, megaphone, cassette recorder, tequila bottle, toy violin, knife, shampoo bottle, etc. The props lie on a table. A digital billboard announces "SPONSORED BY TURISMO FRONTERIZO." On the back wall a pinta reads "Border Brujo (2000 BC–1988)."

INTRODUCTION

[Music plays as the audience enters the space: a collage of Tambora, German punk, bilingual songs from Los Tigres del Norte, and rap opera. Border Brujo organizes the altar table while speaking an Indian dialect. After fixing the altar he grabs the megaphone and switches to English.]

AUTHORITATIVE VOICE
[with megaphone]:
dear audience

feel at home
this continent is your home
grab a cigarette
this is a smoking world
kick back
grab the crotch of your neighbor
& allow me the privilege
of reorganizing your thoughts
dear foreign audience
it's January 1st, 1847
& the U.S. hasn't invaded Mexico yet
this is Mexico carnales!
there is no border
we are merely divided
by the imprecision of your memory
[He enters into a trance, then speaks in tongues. Then he switches to the voice of a drunk.]
DRUNKEN VOICE:
hey, would you leave me alone?
just leave me alone . . .

you're just a border-crosser
a "wetback" with amnesia
who the hell invited your ancestors
to this country by the way?

I

EPIPHANIC VOICE [*eyes closed*]:
I came following your dream
& your dream became my nightmare
once here,
I dreamt you didn't exist
I dreamt a map without borders
where the Latin American archipelago
reached all the way
to the Nuyorrican barrios of Boston and
    Manhattan
all the way to the pockets
of Central American refugees
in Alberta & British Columbia
[*He opens his eyes.*]
& when I dream like this
you suffer
my dream becomes your nightmare
& pot, your only consolation

II

[*Sounds of rooster. Soundtrack: danzon "Imposibile"
by Los Xochimilcas.*]
MEXICAN SOAP-OPERA VOICE
[*parts in Spanish are mispronounced*]:
today, the sun came out in English
the world spins around en inglís
& life is just a melancholic tune
in a foreign tongue . . .
like this one.
[*He shows his tongue to the audience.*]
ay México
Rrrrroooommmantic México
"Amigou Country"
para el gringo desvelado

Tijuana Caliente, la "O"
Mexicali Rose
para el gabacho deshauciado
El Pasou y Juarrézz
ciudades para encontrar el amor
amor que nunca existió
ay México
rrrrooommantic México
paraíso en fragmentación
mariachis desempleados
concheros desnutridos
bandidous alegris
beautiful señoritas
mafioso politicians
federalis que bailan el mambou
el rónchero, la cumbía, la zambía
en-tropical skyline sprayed on the wall
"dare to cross the Tequila border"
dare to cross "the line" without your
Coppertone
transcorporate breeze sponsored by Turismo
maquiladora power for the business macho
crunchy nachos to appease the hunger
[*He turns into a transvestite.*]
TRANSVESTITE VOICE:
Tostada Supreme para aliviar las penas
enchilidas y MacFa-ji-tas
mmmnn . . .
peso little-eat so grandi!
where else but in México

III

[*He manipulates objects from the altar table.*]
NORMAL VOICE:
vivir y crear en California
es un tormento privilegiado
vivir en los '80s
esperar a la muerte total
ser bilingúe, bihemisférico
macizo, sereno, proto-histórico

77

ininteligible luego experi-mental
e incompatible con usted
Señor Monocromatic
víctima del melting plot
[*He turns into a México City ñero* (*derogative for urban mestizo*).]
VOICE OF MEXICO CITY ÑERO:
pinto mi raya
salto la tuya
me dicen el Borges de Caléxico
el Octavio Pus de San Isidro
hablo en español, dígolo intento
& los gabachos me escuchan con recelo
(unos me interrogan con las uñas
y otros me filman en Super-8)

soy posmoderno . . . ¿pos qué?
conceptual . . . ¿con qué?
experi-mental . . . pos qué experi-mentira
mentírame sobre tu pin-che-es-pa-ci-o-cu-pa-do
[*He recites urban jitanjáforas* (*sound poems based on Mexican street voices*).]

IV
[*He begins walking in circles, howling like a wolf, and keeping rhythm with his feet.*]
NORMAL VOICE:
crísis
craises
the biting crises
the barking crises
[*He barks.*]
la crísis es un perro
que nos ladra desde el norte
la crísis es un Chrysler le Baron con 4 puertas
[*He barks again.*]
soy hijo de la crísis fronteriza
soy hijo de la bruja hermafrodita
producto de una cultural cesarean
punkraca heavy-mierda all the way

el chuco funkahuátl desertor de dos paises
rayo tardío de la corriente democratik
vengo del sur
el único de diéz que se pintó
[*He turns into a merolico* (*Mexico City street performer*).]
MEROLICO VOICE [*chanting*]:
nací entre épocas y culturas y vice versa
nací de una herida infectada
herida en llamas
herida que auuuuuulla
[*He howls.*]
I'm a child of border crisis
a product of a cultural cesarean
I was born between epochs & cultures
born from an infected wound
a howling wound
a flaming wound
for I am part of a new mankind
the Fourth World, the migrant kind
los transterrados y descoyuntados
los que partímos y núnca llegamos
y aquí estamos aún
desempleados e incontenibles
en proceso, en ascenso, en transición
per omnia saecula saeculorum
"Invierta en México"
bienes y raíces
vienes y te vas
púdrete a gusto en los United
estate still si no te chingan
[*He finishes with jitanjáforas.*]
VOICE WITH THICK MEXICAN ACCENT
[*pointing at specific audience members*]:
I speak Spanish therefore you hate me
I speak in English therefore they hate me
I speak Spanglish therefore she speaks Ingleñol
I speak in tongues therefore you desire me
I speak to you therefore you kill me
I speak therefore you change

I speak in English therefore you listen
I speak in English therefore I hate you
pero cuando hablo en español te adoro
but when I speak Spanish I adore you

ahora, why carajos do I speak Spanish ?
political praxis craneal
I mean . . .
I mean . . .

V

[*Soundtrack: Supercombo*]
TIJUANA BARKER VOICE [*very fast*]:
welcome to the Casa de Cambio
foreign currency exchange
the Temple of Instant Transformation
the place where Tijuana y San Diego se
    entrepiernan
where the Third becomes the First
and the fist becomes the sphincter
here we produce every imaginable change
money exchange kasse
cambio genético verbal
cambio de dólar y de nombre
cambio de esposa y oficio
de poeta a profeta
de actor a pelotari
de narco a funcionario
de mal en peor
sin cover charge
here everything can take place
for a very very reasonable fee
anything can change into something else
Mexicanos can become Chicanos
overnite
Chicanos become Hispanics
Anglo-Saxons become Sandinistas
& surfers turn into soldiers of fortune
here, fanatic Catholics become swingers
& evangelists go zen
at the snap of my fingers

for a very very modest amount
I can turn your pesos into dollars
your "coke" into flour
your dreams into nightmares
your penis into a clitoris
you name it, Califa
if your name is Guillermo Gómez-Peña
I can turn it into Guermo Comes Penis
or Bill, "the multimedia beaner"
or even better, Indocumentado #00281431
because here Spanish becomes English,
    ipso facto
& life becomes art with the same speed
that mambo becomes jazz
tostadas become pizza
machos become transvestitas
& brujos become performance artists
it's fun, it's fast
it's easy, it's worthwhile
you just gotta cross the border
[*He stands and performs a biblical gesture.*]
¡Lázaro gabacho wake up and cross!
crossss . . . cruzzzzz . . . crasssss

VI

[*He begins the following text with a psalm in Latin.
He delivers text like a Catholic chant.*]
Cyber-Bwana
Tezocatlipoca Electronic
Fabricante de la Imágen Internacional
Padrasto de la Incertidumbre Mundial
Legislador de la Tercera y Ultima Realidad
Gran Mano que todo lo acorrala
you ordered us to come
via TV via rock & roll
Imevisíon here we are
SPANISH INTERNATIONAL NETWORK
& here we are . . .
to stay
[*He continues with norteño (Northern Mexican)
accent.*]

NORTEÑO VOICE:
Cyber-Bwana
we are your product in a way
we are what you can only dream about
we hold the tiny artery
which links you to the past
the umbilical cord that goes back to the origins
from Homo Punk to Homo Pre-Hispanic
from high-tech to Aztec without missing a beat
without us you would go mad
without us you would forget who you really are
without us you are just another tourist lost in
    Puerto Vallarta
[*He grabs megaphone.*]
we perform, we scold you, we remind you
'cause we are so little
so fuckin' minute
what else can we do?

VII

[*Soundtrack: Tambora Sinaloense*]
DRUNKEN VOICE:
. . . & you think we have nothing in common?
well, well
you are a victim of your government
& so am I . . . of yours
I am here 'cause your government
went down there
to my country
without a formal invitation
& took all our resources
so I came to look for them
just to look for them
nothing else
[*He drinks from the shampoo bottle.*]
if you see a refugee tonight
treat him well
he's just seeking his stolen resources
if you happen to meet a migrant worker
treat him well
he's merely picking the food

that was stolen from his garden
[*He begins to scream.*]
has anyone seen my stolen resources?
has anyone seen my coffee,
my copper, my banana, my gas,
my cocaine, my wrestling mask?
my my ma-ma, ma-ma-cita . . . ¡mamita!
[*He cries.*]

VIII

AUTHORITATIVE VOICE [*with megaphone*]:
dear Californian
we harvest your food
we cook it
& serve it to you
we sing for you
we fix your car
we paint your house
we trim your garden
we babysit your children
and now
we even tell you what to do:
go South, Califa
abandon your dream
& join the continental project
dear Californian,
your hours are counted
on the fingers of your unwillingness
to become part of the world
you must be scared shitless of the future
[*He speaks in tongues.*]
I've got the future in my throat
[*He speaks in tongues.*]
take me or kill me, Pochtlani
look South or go mad
I mean it, vato
[*He speaks in tongues.*]
. . . & you dare to ask me
where I have been
all these years?

IX

VULNERABLE AND TENDER VOICE:
estimado compañero
del otro lado del espejo
there's really no danger tonight
estoy completamente desarmado
the only real danger lies
in your inability to understand me
in your unwillingness to trust
the only real danger is in your fingers
your thumb lies on the button
your index finger on the trigger
you have the weapons maestro
I merely have the word
my tongue is licking your wounds
it hurts but it makes sense
it's up to you to dialogue
it's up to you to dialogue

X

[*Soundtrack: Ry Cooder. He speaks like a smooth-talker, and sends kisses to various audience members.*]
SMOOTH-TALKER VOICE:
smack! smack!
hey baby . . . baby, güerita
duraznito en almíbar, nalguita descolorida
It's me, the Mexican beast
we are here to talk, to change, to ex-change
to ex-change images and fluids
to look at each other's eyes
to look at each other's mmmhhj
so let's pull down the zipper of our fears
& begin the . . . Binational Summit mi vida
but remember,
I'm not your tourist guide across the
    undetermined otherness
this ain't no tropical safari to Palenke or
    Martinique
much less a private seminar on interracial
    relations

[*He changes to normal voice.*]
NORMAL VOICE:
this is a basic survival proposal
from a fellow Mex-american
in the debris of continental culture
& all this blood is real
the hoopla is false but the blood is real
come taste it mi amor
[*He grabs the megaphone.*]
AUTHORITATIVE VOICE [*with megaphone*]:
subtext:
dear border lover
Eurídice Anglosajona
the state of interracial communication
has been seriously damaged by the AIDS crisis
we are no longer fucking our brains out
no longer masturbating across the fence
no longer exchanging binational fluids
we are merely stalking & waiting
waiting for better times
& more efficient medication
we are horny & scared
very horny & very scared
tonight we must look for other strategies
& place additional importance on the word
I love you querida amante extranjera
but this time you have to be content with my
    words
la palabra alivia las heridos de la historia

XI

[*He speaks in broken English.*]
no, I did not qualify
my ex-landlord didn't recognize me when
    I called
my employers said they'd never seen me before
those art lords didn't want to sign the form
"there's no recognizable form in your art"
    — they said
"there's no recognizable form for your fear"
    — I told them

"your aggressivity is an expression of cultural
   weakness" — they replied
"but which is the form of my dignity?"
   — I asked rhetorically
[*Pause*]
They were shocked by how articulate I was
[*Voice becomes softer.*]
form, form
form without content
love without saliva
art without ideas
tacos without salsa
life without redemption
form, form, form, conform
[*Voice changes to stylized Pachuco.*]
PACHUCO VOICE:
form a coalition carnal i
no te duermas Samurai i
get a computer pirata i
but buzo
if your umbilical cord breaks
there's nothing we can do
you're gone
lost in the all-encompassing fog
of the United States of America
& then
you es-tass jou-didou
com-pre-hen-di?
[*He continues in a normal voice.*]
NORMAL VOICE:
The day I was born
September 23 of 1955
eternity died
& the border wound became infected
the day my father died
February 17 of 1989
my last tentacle with México broke
& I finally became a Chicano

XII
[*He holds the Tequila bottle and delivers the follow-
ing commercial as a Latino transvestite.*]
TRANSVESTITE VOICE:
Tequila Güero . . . with menthol
the new breath of old México
for the contemporary warrior
who doesn't want to give up
his language, his identity or his . . . mmhhjj
[*He proceeds to advertise the shampoo bottle in an
Indian dialect.*]

XIII
[*Soundtrack: "La Negra" fading in and out. He
clearly experiences a lot of pain.*]
AGITATED VOICE:
¡ay!
¡¡ayy!!
¡¡¡aayyy!!!
las leyes que emasculan
la orden mortal en forma de cupón
de imágen televisiva
. . . trémula voz eléctrica
al otro lado del teléfono
95-619 . . .
al otro lado del other side
[*He grabs the telephone handset, and parodies a
Mexican accent.*]
VOICE WITH MEXICAN ACCENT:
hellou, hellou
alo Jack
can you hearr me?
can you rreally hear me?
I am finally speakin' English
. . . no, no, you are not to blame
for the invasion of Grenada . . .
the air raid on Libya wasn't your fault . . .
the Iran-Contra aid wasn't really your initiative
nor were the last economic sanctions against
   México
[*He pauses.*]

Jack, you have delusions of grandeur
you were merely receiving instructions
. . . & please forgive my bad English
I came too old to this country
& I haven't been domesticated yet
[*He hangs up the telephone.*]
NORMAL VOICE:
the Marine stood up
kicked the table
spit in my face
"you goddamn terrorist wetback!"
& began to cry like a Chihuahua
[*He pauses.*]
. . . but the mariachis never stopped playing
they are still playing right now
what a beautiful paradox
California sinks
& the mariachis keep playing
can you hear them?
can you really hear them?

XIV

AUTHORITATIVE VOICE [*with megaphone*]:
Hello, this is authentic Latino performance art
zero bullshit/lots of style
[*He puts on shaman wig, delivers text with a
breathy drunken voice.*]
DRUNKEN VOICE:
I am 33, the age of Christ
& this is the year of Armageddon
the "Year of the Yellow Spider"
according to the Tasadays
& the Chinese "Year of the Snake"
digo la neta es que
your president & bunch have brought
sadness, radioactivity, & death
to the whole damn world
[*He burps and coughs.*]
they've killed thousands of people
down south & overseas
& you are also responsible

come dice Chomsky
"we are all responsible
for the crimes of our governments . . ."
but . . .
you are particularly responsible
for the crimes of the CIA, the FBI,
the Border Patrol, the Contras . . .
you are responsible for all civilian mercenaries
engaged in foreign causes
both military & artistic
you are also responsible for . . .
[*Pause*]
why are you responsible?
[*He answers in an Indian dialect, then continues as
a hipster.*]
HIPSTER VOICE:
hey, I grow the pot . . . & you smoke it
I need dollars, you need magic
a perfect transaction I'd say
we both need to overcome our particular
    devaluations, que no?

XV

[*Soundtrack: Gregorian chants*]
TV EVANGELIST VOICE:
you can leave this space if you wish
there's really nowhere else to go
your house has been culturally occupied
your mind is already invaded
trust me
let's begin to talk
let's stop performing
this is an art of emergency
there's nowhere else to go
the South is in flames
the border has been cancelled
& the North is occupied
by Reagan's conceptual battalion
I'm sorry for being so direct
but we are running out of time, pesos & faith
we are running out of time, pesos & faith

we are running out of time, pesos & faith
we are running out of time, pesos & faith . . .

XVI
CANTINFLAS-LIKE VOICE [*very fast*]:
they say I talk to gringos
they say I wasn't born in East L.A.
they say I left the Committee by choice
they say I promote "negative stereotypes" of my
   people
they say I sound like Pablo Neruda gone punk
they say my art is a declaration
against the Holy Virgin of Mexican aesthetics
they say my politics are endangering the Party
they say I'm sleeping with a post-structuralist
   feminist troublemaker
they say I have to stop riding my experimental
   donkey
and put my feet on the ground
once and for all
but let me tell you something
I feel no ground under my feet
I'm floating, floating
on the ether
of the present tense
of California
and the past tense
of Mexico
[*He speaks in tongues.*]

XVII
NORMAL VOICE:
. . . porque sufro la gran ruptura
fractura parietal en 5º grado
Estar dos Unidas es pura ilusión
. . . porque sufro el gran destierro
la vida es un lento destierro
good-bye compadre transhumante
Ulises ranchero
te apaño la migra por 9a ocasión
te quedaste sin cruzar

sin cruisin' no hay redemption
somos nadie enel éter desunidos
en USA desunidos
mita y míto
partidos por la mitad
[*He grabs a knife, gestures as though wanting to
commit hara-kiri. He speaks like a macuarro (racist
depiction of a Mexico City urban mestizo).*]
MACUARRO VOICE:
soy carne de cañón
papel de hoguera
ardo en las llamas del arte contemporáneo
arde el inglés en mi garganta
arde el D.F. en mi memoria
arde la llama del movimiento
apenas
apenas
apenitas
[*He stabs himself.*]
aaaaaagggggggghhhhhhhh
[*He continues with a normal voice.*]
NORMAL VOICE:
& as I was crossing the border checkpoint
this somewhat intelligent migra
confiscated a copy of this text
he read a few pages
& asked if I was a member
of the Partido Chicano-Cardenista
"no, señor," I replied
"I am a member of the Tribe of the Inflamed
   Eyelids"
he tore my passport in half
& I proceeded to kick him in the balls
for the sake of experimentation
I mean, for the sake of experimentation

XVIII
[*Soundtrack: cumbia. He speaks like a Tijuana
street hustler.*]
STREET-HUSTLER VOICE:
hey mister . . . mixter

& you thought Mexico was South America?
& you thought Castillian Spanish was better
   than Mexican
you thought salsa was Mexican music
you thought all Mexicans were dark-skinned
& short & talkative like me
you thought Mexican art was a bunch of candy
   skulls & velvet paintings
you thought Mexico represented your past
& now you're realizing Mexico is your future
you thought there was a border between the 1st
   & the 3rd worlds
& now you're realizing you're part of the 3rd
   world
& your children are hanging out with us
& your children & us are plotting against you
hey mister, eeeh mister . . . mister
& suddenly you woke up
& it was too late to call the priest, the cops or
   the psychiatrist
ay, qué pinche sustote te pegaste
y en español

XIX
[*He grabs the megaphone.*]
AUTHORITATIVE VOICE [*with megaphone*]:
hello, this is the uncensored voice of the "Latino
boom":
I mean to ask you some questions
dear curator
dear collector
dear candidate
dear anthropologist
where can we draw the line between curiosity &
   exploitation?
between dialogue & entertainment?
between democratic participation & tokenism?
where is the borderline
between my Spanish & your English?
ce n'est pas ici

between my sperm & your mouth
there is a cultural void
between my wings & your knife
there's uncontrollable panic
between my words & your ears
there are 33 years of rain
& between my art & yours
there's 10,000 miles of misunderstanding
[*He subvocalizes, speaks in an Indian dialect, then
nonchalantly continues text.*]
what I think is avant-garde, you think is passé
what I think is cool, you think is corny
what I think is funny, you think is cruel
what I think is fascism, you think is just life
what I think is life, you think is romantic
what I think is true, you think is literature
what I think is art, you just have no time for it
what I think is West, you think is South
what I think is America, you think is your
   country
[*He stands up and screams.*]
we are so far away from one another
we are so far away from one another!!
[*He mouths as if screaming, then continues text in a
cool style.*]
I speak therefore you misinterpret me
I am in Tijuana, you are in ... [*city in which he is
performing*]
I exist therefore you misunderstand me
I walk back into Spanish
for there are many concepts to protect
good-bye compita
extranjero en tu propio país
chao, chaocito, adieu
auf Wiedersehen, caput, puut'íssimus . . .
[*He performs "offensive" Mexican street sign lan-
guage. Lights fade out.*]

INTERMISSION

XX

[*Soundtrack: bullfight music*]

MEROLICO VOICE:

so, ¿a qué vienes extranjero?

¿a experimentar "peligro cultural?"

¿a tocarle los pies al brujo?

¿a pedirle perdón?

¿a ver si te reorienta hacia el poniente?

pero sus palabras te confunden aún más

te hieren, te desconsuelan

you can't even understand the guy

'cause he speaks in a foreign tongue

seems real angry & ungrateful

& you begin to wonder

REDNECK VOICE

[*mumbling and mispronouncing Spanish*]:

whatever happened to the sleepy Mexican

the smiley guy you met last summer

on the "Amigou Country" cruise, remember?

whatever happened to the great host

the helpful kimozabe

the sexy mariachi with pencil mostachio

the chubby cartoon character

you enjoyed so much in last Sunday's paper?

whatever happened to Speedy González

Fritou Banditou, Johnny McTaco, Pancho de
   Nacho,

los treis caballerous, Ricardou Mont'lban

the Baja Marimba Band y sus cantina girls?

when did they disappear?

were they deported back to Mexicorama?

how? through Mexicannabis Airlines

& who let these troublemakers in?

are they for real? 'cause . . .

I want to witness a real representation

NORMAL VOICE:

hmmm, how ironic

I represent you

yet, you don't represent me

& you think you still have the power to define?

please . . .

please . . .

please . . .

XXI

[*He speaks elegantly and with a soft-spoken
manner.*]

PACHUCO DANDY VOICE:

please don't touch me

I've got typhoid & malaria

don't you dare touch me

I haven't been documented yet

I'm still an illegal alien

my back is wet

my nipples are hard

I'm ready to fight

I'm ready to rape

don't like me too much

'cause I'm a drug-smuggling

welfare recipient-to-be

sexist communist car thief

fanatically devoted to the overthrow

of the U.S. government & the art world

[*He pauses.*]

no, just kiddin'

don't listen to me

I'm just a deterritorialized "chilango"

who claims to be a Chicano

& I'm not even eligible for amnesty

'cause I never documented my work

the only photos of my performances

are in the archives of the FBI

& I'm a bit too shy to ask them for copies

can anyone document me please?

can anyone take a photo of this memorable
   occasion?

[*Pause*]

come on, for the archives of border culture

for the history of performance art

can anyone be so kind as to authenticate my
   existence?
[*He freezes for twenty seconds.*]

XXII
[*Soundtrack: old instrumental blues*]
MACUARRO VOICE:
cameras 1 & 2 rolling
¡música maestro!
[*Music doesn't start.*]
¡música! pss, ¿que pasó? . . . pos nos la echamos
   sin música
[*Music finally begins.*]
I was born in the middle of a movie set
they were shooting "La Migra Contra El
   Príncipe Chichimeca"
I was literally born in the middle of a battle
I'm almost an aborigine you know
a Hollywood Indian, ¡ajjuua!
me dicen el Papantla Flyer
de la Broadway, bien tumbado
'cause I love to show my balls to strangers
& to talk dirty to gringas feministas
& if it wasn't for the fact that I've read
too much Foucault & Baudrillard
& Fuentes & Subirats & Roger Bartra
& other writers you haven't even heard of
I could fulfill your expectations much better
if it wasn't for the fact that I wrote
this text on a Macintosh
& I couldn't even memorize it all
& I shot my rehearsals with a Sony-8
I would really fulfill your expectations
le bon sauvage du Mexique
l'enfant terrible de la frontière

XXIII
[*Soundtrack: Ry Cooder's "Canción Mixteca." He
speaks with an unbearably snobbish accent.*]
UPPER-CLASS LATINO VOICE:
oui, oui, oui

Mexique ooh la la
Chingada da-da
les enfants de la chingada
México rrromantic México
paraíso para tizos
para todos tifoidea
Chili Ortega pa'la güera
muchiou machou el muchiachou
ay, que rrico gaspachou
oh, pardon
don Giovani tampocou Mexicani?
from where?
São Paolo, Manila, or Cuernavaca ?
[*He changes voice to that of a drunken tourist.*]
DRUNKEN-TOURIST VOICE:
well, I don't care
it's all the same
the world is filled with colorful creatures
like me, like them
I simply adore Mexico
its fleshy señoritas
with humongous black eyes
walking down Revolución
like hundreds of Carmen Mirandas
with sombrero grandi & Coppertone
& man, they sure don't complain about
   machismo
they love it!!
porqui let's face it
el machou Mexicanou no ser tan machou como
   el Texanou

XXIV
UPPER-CLASS LATINO VOICE [*super-flam-
boyantly and with exaggerated gestures*]:
please, check my pronounciation
I'm a child of the fallen Latin American
   oligarchy

I dream of a beautiful, beautiful condo
in Coronado or Key West

away from my homeland in turmoil
I dream of a disinfected environment
one that only my memory can inhabit
& only the memories I want
she dreams of a beautiful suburb
[*He points at an audience member.*]
somewhere in the periphery of her fears
she's tired of suffering
she lost her man in Santiago
her son in Guatemala
her daughter raped by a U.S. Marine
she walked all the way from Tegucigalpa
she came to ask for an explanation
can anyone explain to her why?

XXV

[*He switches to a redneck accent, speaks through a megaphone.*]
REDNECK VOICE:
"no, no, too didactic" . . .
too romantic, too, too . . .
[*He barks.*]
not experimental enough
not inter-dizzy enough
[*He barks again.*]
looks like . . .
[*He barks.*]
old-fashioned Anglo stuff
I mean not enough . . . picante
not enough bravadou & passionadou
I want mucho more
I want to see García Márquez in 3-D
a post-posty rendition of Castañeda
holographic shamans flying onstage
political massacres on multiple screens
[*He gets progressively crazier.*]
what's wrong with you pre-technological
    creatures ?!
a-ffir-ma-ti-ve-ac-tion-pimps!
you can't even put together a good fuckin'
    video!!

[*He breathes heavily and rests his head on the table.*]

XXVI

[*Pre-recorded text in an Indian language continues throughout the following section.*]
NEWSCASTER VOICE [*with an artificial smile*]:
please, check my pronunciation
this is the year of the Hispanic
Hispanics on MTV
Hispanics on Broadway
Hispanics in Hollywood
Hispanics in the Museum of Modern Art
Hispanics on video
Hispanics in the Calendar Section
Hispanics in Ripley's Believe It Or Not
Hispanics in Congress
Hispanics in General Dynamics
Hispanics in the Border Patrol
Hispanics in Federal Jail
Hispanics on Skid Row
Hispanics in AIDS clinics
Hispanics in the cemetery
Hispanics in different sizes
buy one/get one free
it's in, it's hot, it's cheap, it's durable
& like the bumper sticker says
"A true Hispanic is not just your panic,
but everyone's panic."
[*He pauses.*]
as I was saying
thanks to marketing
& not to civil rights
we are the new generation
[*He pauses.*]
of laboratory rats & experimental patients.
[*He begins to cut coke and speak like a druggie.*]
. . . at night
alone in my condo
when I pray to my 3-D virgin

it's strange you know
I'm happy yet I feel like killing myself
so I take more pills to fall asleep
the pills you sent me last month are terrific
they make me forget all the pain
& alienation I thought I used to feel
they make me feel part of it all
with them I feel one with California
one with the art world
& a thousand within myself
justo a tu imágen y semejanza
so I turn on the radio . . .

XXVII
AUTHORITATIVE VOICE [*with megaphone*]:
alien-ation
alien action
alienated
álguien ate it
alien hatred
aliens out there
hay álguien out there
Aliens the movie
Aliens the album
Cowboys vs. Aliens
Bikers vs. Aliens
The Wetback from Mars
*The Mexican Transformer & his Radio-active
   Torta*
The Conquest of Tenochtitlan by Spielberg
The Reconquest of Aztlán by Monty Python
The Brown Wave vs. the Micro Wave
Invaders from the South vs. the San Diego Padres
reinforced by the San Diego Police
reinforced by your ignorance dear San Diegan...

good morning
this is Radio Latino FM
spoiling your breakfast as always
[*The remainder of this text is pre-recorded. He
sub-vocalizes.*]

efectivamente, anoche asesinaron
a un niño mexicano de escasos 8 años
la patrulla fronteriza asegura
que se trata de "peligroso asaltante"
a continuación, más noticias en inglés:

the Mexican fly is heading north
the Mexican fly is coming to destroy your crops
the Mexican fly is now in Chihuahua
there's no insecticide for the Mexican fly
no antidote for your fear of otherness
the Simpson-Rodino bill is an emergency plan
   to regulate your fears
some call it an act of political fumigation
the Amnesty Program has been designed to
   legalize otherness
for otherness keeps leaking into the country
into your psyche

dear listener/dear audience
your country is no longer yours
your relationship with otherness has reached a
   point of crisis
you love me/you hate me
you are in good company
but you don't know it yet
the Mexican fly will be coming soon to a garden
   near you
good evening
this is Radio Latino FM
interrupting your coitus as always
[*He sings an Indian song and covers his face with
the hair of the wig.*]

XXVIII
[*Soundtrack: New Age percussion. He enters into
a trance.*]
I see Tenochtitlán Island
resting peacefully on the surface of a daiquiri
I see the Aztec warrior in a straitjacket
facing a 100-year sentence in Chino

I see the Spanish landowner & the American
tourist
getting wasted at Margarita's Village
I see the border guards masturbating & vomiting
under the border fog
under the very fog that covers us right now
I see the first sparks of the 2nd Mexican
    Independence
& the final kicks of a drowning saurus
I see other more personal things
like friendly women & friendly men
really trying to understand
but despite all of these visions
estoy triste en país ajeno
estoy muy triste en país ajeno
estamos tristes en país ajeno
país de todos/país de nadie
& there's nothing you can do to ease my pain
nothing sadder than a Mexican artist in
    Southern California
under the present Administration
nothing is really administered but death
[*He speaks in tongues.*]
I mean, death as a "lifestyle"
death as a media celebrity
death as a mandatory practice
la gran calaca güera que todo lo gobierna
[*He speaks in tongues.*]
in order to operate without physical
    repercussions
I chose the temporary safety of the art world
[*He continues to speak in tongues.*]

XXIX
[*He screams over the heads of the audience, as if
wanting to reach someone far away.*]
hermano de allá
de hasta allá abajo
si tan sólo supieras lo que es
pasarse una noche solitaria
en un motel de Alabama

en una cantina de Oxnard o Detroit
caminar por las calles desiertas y peligrosas
de Marin County o Pasadena
amar en Nueva York
con el temor de un contagio mortal
y por si fuera poco
sentir la lúz del helicóptero en Imperial Beach
la voz forastera por la espalda . . .
[*He freezes for twenty seconds.*]

XXX
BROKEN-ENGLISH VOICE:
no, I have no green card
I was illegally hired by this gallery
the director might receive employer's sanctions
the INS might raid my audience
one of these nights
one of them might even shoot me
from the audience
perhaps tonight
one never knows nowadays
anything can happen in America
we are so fuckin' vulnerable in America
I'm scared therefore you exist
so look out for mei
I'm going through the Big Smokei
I'm going through the Big Smokei
& so are you
[*He walks through the audience while speaking
in tongues. He suddenly stops, and seems very
irritated.*]
there is a Border Patrol agent in the audience
can he please identify himself?
can you please identify yourself?
[*Long pause*]
¡cobarde!

XXXI
AUTHORITATIVE VOICE [*with megaphone*]:
[*He points with a flashlight at the faces of audience
members.*]

dear friends

let me ask you a few questions

has anyone ever crossed a border illegally?

has anyone ever smuggled any "illegal sub-
stances" or radical literature?

have you ever harbored or hired an "illegal
alien"?

have you ever worked illegally yourself?

have you ever visited a "communist country" or
a transvestite cantina?

have you ever joined an anti-American organiza-
tion named. . . ?

have you ever engaged in sexually illicit
practices?

come on, be honest

this is just a performance

no big deal

I've been asked myself each of these questions

at least a couple hundred times

& I've been violently frisked at least 20 times

for not having answered them

[*He puts down the megaphone, raises his hands,
and freezes.*]

& you ask me

"are you implying that the U.S. is a police
state?"

but I can only answer in náhuatl

[*He answers in an Indian dialect.*]

but you insist

"isn't California the ultimate utopia for Latinos?"

& this time I answer with a violent question

"isn't Disneyland the capital of California?"

& you interrupt me with a knife

". . . but Guillermo, you're cheating

you're exercising your political freedom"

& I think for a second, "hmmm"

& reply "sure . . ."

but how many people are here tonight

to listen to my political freedom?

& we begin to count them

& as we count them in Spanish

we begin to wonder about freedom in America

& the show goes on

& the critic over there is falling asleep

wondering why Latinos are so bloody dramatic

XXXII

[*He lights a joint and speaks as though he were
"high."*]

STONED VOICE:

our moment arrived

we did have a chance to speak out

but we hesitated

& someone up there

unplugged the lights . . . & the cameras

before we even realized it

[*He smokes more pot. His voice becomes muddy.*]

the "quebequization" of the Southwest

was effectively co-opted by the NSA

& our communities were fragmented

by the asymmetrical distribution of funding &
space

we all know it . . .

we all suffer it

[*He snorts fictional drugs. He speaks like a junkie,
moving his head like a pendulum.*]

JUNKIE VOICE:

today, once again

we are alone

like in the early days

alone like children in the forest

like Chicano performance artists

in Anglo alternative spaces

we are alone & waiting

like the popular corrido says

"some are waiting for Amnesty

& others for the guillotine blade"

[*He repeats this phrase several times as if totally
drugged out. Then he puts on a wrestler's mask and
stands up.*]

XXXIII
VOICE OF HARD-CORE POLITICAL
ACTIVIST:
"whatever happened to the leaders?" you ask me
some died of a heart attack
with a little help from the CIA
some are mortally wounded by the media
& others paralyzed by chemical nostalgia
a few created an impenetrable bureaucracy
emulating their enemies
or found refuge & comfort in the university spa
today, [date]
standing on the edge
of the 20th-century cliff
I finally dare to ask you
where are all my Chicano compadres?
I can't accept that they all went crazy like me
or yuppie like some of you
can't accept that the Indian leaders are still in jail
can't believe that the Puerto Rican independen-
    tistas are still in jail
after all these years
still in jail in America
& you worry about Nelson Mandela?
[Long pause]
& you worry about Lech Walesa?
[Long pause]
& you worry about cigarette smoking?
[He cries for a few seconds, then covers his face.]

XXXIV
[He continues like a hard-core political activist.]
last night at the "Main Intersection"
someone told me
that all we want is
access to the suburbs
access to the museums
to the city council
to the media
to your girlfriend
that all-we-want-is-access

access!, access!, access!!
well, I'm sorry to disappoint you, "someone"
all we want is to go back
but for the moment
there's nowhere to go back to
[He pauses.]
our past was destroyed by your government
therefore, dear "someone"
this is our land for the moment
& you gotta share the pie
to regain your peace of mind
[He speaks in tongues.]
& you insist on asking me
what I'm doing here?
como podré explicártelo
sin ofenderte...
if Spalding Gray can go to Cambodia
why can't I come to [city where he is performing]?

XXXV
[Soundtrack: Rossini or Beethoven]
AUTHORITATIVE VOICE [with megaphone]:
tonight, I am the one who determines
the exact nature of our relation
even if only for one night
I say:
you are no longer my spectator
you are my object of adoration
your country is losing weight & size
your skin is losing its privilege
your crisis is graver than mine
I say:
ciudadano del mentado primer mundo
you have a friend in me
a solid but critical friend
a friend who will never betray you
but never again will accept
your asymmetrical conditions
I say:
generic citizenry
Norteamérica has grown

back to its original size
from Yucatán to Greenland
from Michigan to Michoacán
I toast to Nuestra América
from the Papago to the punk
I toast to the beginning of an era
a true multicultural society
from ritual art to "neo-geo"
I toast in equal terms with you
my dear Anglosaxican partner
waspano de tercera generación
in my performance country
República de Arteamérica
you're just a minority
but you have some rights
like the right to listen respectfully
& as long as you continue
to fear moi or desire me
without proportion to my dignity
then, my dear involuntary neighbor
entropy will keep creeping
like magma into your home
into your troubled spirit
& I won't be there to rescue you
from the flood of your guilt
[*He puts down the megaphone.*]

XXXVI
[*Soundtrack: "Ojos Españoles" by Los Xochimilcas.
He applies orange or red makeup while speaking.*]
SMOOTH-TALKER VOICE:
so, my dear audience
we are finally in the same room
even if only for an evening
we are truly conversing right now
in your language,
but conversing after all . . .
so I mean to ask you
where is the threshhold of your desire?

Baghdad, São Paulo, Berlin, Tangiers,
Calcutta, Tijuana, Ibiza, La Chingada?
where are your memories running loose?
in which bed
in whose arms
on which stage
in which language are you dreaming?
in Spanish, Jamaican English, or Persian?
where will your permanent home be erected?
in Jakarta, Managua, or Oro Preto
perhaps somewhere on the shores of Cataluña
beyond the borders of panic & boredom?
I envy your capability to desire
I really do
DRUNKEN VOICE:
I'm here in prison
right in the center of the wound
right in the crack of the 2 countries
I am a prisoner of thought
a prisoner of art
a prisoner of a media war
I'm each & every bad guy in the film
a one-man film so to speak
they call me El Corny, El Slickoid
El Nahuál Conceptual, El Suddenly Violento
El Channy Fumigamitos
I'm getting tired, corazón
where demonios are you?
I want to read you something from my heart
[*Screaming*]
are you coming to visit me tonight?
are they going to let you in?!

XXXVII
[*Music continues. He speaks like a stylized
Pachuco.*]
PACHUCO VOICE:
hey!
my Spider Babe
my Surfin' Loca

my Mambo Jane
my Bless Me Ultima
la Jazzercise
házmela buena
la Nena Radioactiva
la Biker Lacandona
la Corporate Chingona
la búscame a horcajadas en noches de neón
la gimme those besitos across the border fence
ay, ay, Pantera Feminista
la gran Bruja Marxista
abráxame retuérxeme
soy tu loco encaramado al muslo izquierdo
y no me suelto por nada
soy el pendejo permanente
que llevas tatuado en una chichi
la izquierda, la grandota
y no me borro
ay, Batichica de Mexicali
let me know if you are coming back soon
for I'm tired of fighting la migra by myself
ay, my little brown self
is almost non-existent tonight
ay, la pinche velita se me apaga
la pinche velita se me apaga
[*He blows out the candles one by one.*]

XXXVIII

[*He drinks from shampoo bottle. While speaking, he covers his face with his hands.*]
DRUNKEN VOICE:
I hate to say it but we failed
[*He pauses.*]
we are still alive but . . . we failed
still awake, sort of

but kind'a clumsy & fuzzy
the food tastes like shit
the music is awful
it's all been done before
one artist replaces the other
one minority replaces the other
& the other, other, other, others
next year Latinos are "out"
& albino Romanians are "in"
therefore my dear audience
I'm going back to Hell
en camión de tres estrellas
como vine
back to the origins maextro

XXXIX

[*He begins to walk into the audience. He holds two baskets: one is empty, and the other is filled with food and ritual objects.*]
CANTINFLAS-LIKE VOICE [*very fast*]:
but before I go back
ladies & gentlemen
I'm going to ask you to give me
whatever you no longer need
please feel free to get rid of everything
you wish you didn't have:
money, IDs, ideas, your keys, your sins
your telephone number, your credit card
your leather jacket, your contact lenses, etc.
please make sure that whatever you give me
you're prepared to never see again
some objects I will bury right in the
    U.S./México border ditch
& others will become part of my traveling alta
damas y caballeros . . . ¡aflojen!

FIN

AMERICA

2000 YEARS

OF DREAMING

500 YEARS OF

NIGHTMARE

1992
A PERFORMANCE CHRONICLE
OF THE RE-DISCOVERY OF AMERICA
BY
"THE WARRIOR FOR GRINGOSTROIKA"

PROGRAM NOTES

This performance trilogy is my humble contribution to the collective project of re-defining what is mistakenly called "the discovery of America." The notion of discovery functions as a euphemism for the genocide and domination that made America into the United States, and Latin America into a subsidiary of Europe. This notion has to be challenged and re-defined.

1992 is also a disnarrative reflection of my life as a child of many cultures and epochs; the life of my original community, the Mexicans outside Mexico; and the poetical history of my lost generation, the beloved Tribe of the Fiery Pupils.

In this multiple journey through my three decades of life and America's last 500 years, I zigzag from the past to the future and from the personal to the historical, in hopes of shedding light on our contemporary experience as multi-, inter-, and trans-cultural citizens of a country that has ferociously resisted accepting its mestizo condition and multiracial soul.

I also hope to express the fact that Mexican and therefore Chicano culture, since the much-touted discovery, and more recently since the transfer of territory in 1848, has been the result of an ongoing clash of disparate cultures. And we have learned to live within this syncretism. As Mexicans we are crucified by the North, the South, the East, and the West. We are Indian, mestizo, and Spanish (therefore also Arabic). Many of our paisanos have African, European, or Jewish blood. And since the 1950s, today more than ever, U.S. pop culture has penetrated every aspect of our lives via TV, tourism, rock and roll, fashion, and food. Though the other is always inside of us, Anglo culture has managed to make us a double other, within and outside. This text will function as a mirror between the two.

As a cross-cultural artist, my aesthetics are from many traditions that are equidistant, and that I wish to acknowledge. Among others, border art, Chicano literature, the Mexico City post-earthquake rock-and-roll movement, experimental cinema, "border blaster" radio, and the U.S. performance-art-monologue movement.

All characters and voices are performed by myself.

Depending on the cultural context and/or availability of resources, every piece can be shorter or longer, more or less complex technically, more or less humorous, confrontational or stylized.

Notes on the Voices: The texts in Spanish and Spanglish must not be translated. The "nasal voice" is like the voice of a 1940s radio announcer. The "tongues" are a personal "esperanto" that experiments with the phonetic structures of indigenous language, and sounds like shamanistic tongues. The "Cabaret Animateur" sounds like the flamboyant announcer in a border nightclub. The "merolico" is a Mexican street vendor. "El Piporro" is a famous movie star and singer. The "norteño," "pinto," "pachuco," and "ñero" accents are stylizations of stereotypical personae. The "grinoñol" is a caricature of the accent of American tourists. The megaphone creates both a dramatic distance and a sense of political authority. Other voices and accents are self-explanatory.

The text is never "finished." I constantly rewrite it and add the new elements I come across while performing in different contexts. This publication is just one version. The piece has been performed in the United States, Mexico, Canada, England, Belgium, Italy, and the Soviet Union. Excerpts have also appeared on public access TV and National Public Radio as well as on Mexican Radio Education.

A POEM FOR THE PROGRAM
[*El Aztec High-Tech presents the opening remarks at the Multicultural Peace Conference. Hybrids and essentialists listen carefully:*]
"during my exorbitant journey

beyond the limits of Western culture
I learned a few things
from quite respectable individuals
the Mexico City bums taught me to walk
    without leaving a footprint
the Chamula Indians taught me to curse the
    divinity when necessary
the Huicholes taught me to lose control without
    losing my dignity
the merolicos taught me to besiege my audience
    with words
the Chicanos taught me to articulate my pain
with maximum quality and a minimum of
    resources
my black colleagues taught me to detect the spiders of racism on the spot
my red colleagues taught me to remain still in
    the face of danger
my feminist comadres taught me to distrust men
without visible weaknesses

tonight I put all this knowlege on a plate
& serve it to you with all my affection
eat, my dear colleagues, eat!
[*Two hours later, all uninvited guests begin to die from food poisoning.*]

I

[*In the center of stage, there is a table with a chair, a mike, and a music stand; and in front, a semicircle of votive candles. A small coffee table to the right of the chair acts as a prop and costume table. Props include: a megaphone, a knife, a rubber heart, 1950s-style sunglasses, a wrestler mask, a Pachuco hat, an Indian headdress, a wooden snake, and a shampoo bottle. Several dead chickens hang from the ceiling at different heights.*]

LA PARTIDA ORIGINAL
NASAL VOICE [*with megaphone*]:
in August of 1492

Columbus departed from the Port of Palos
in 3 state-of-the-art carabelas.
La Pinta for the prisoners
La Niña for the child molesters
y la Santa María for the religious fanatics
Columbus arrived in America without papers
don't we all secretly wish he had been deported
   right away?
NORMAL VOICE:
in August of 1942
my uncle Pepe departed from Mexico City
with 100 pesos in his pocket
he arrived in Los Angeles without papers
& became a clothing designer for prominent
   Pachucos
don't we all wish he dies in peace?
pazzz, pastiche . . .
partir
de una lengua a otra
de una ciudad a otro país
a otro continente o sueño
partimos
y en proceso de estallar
estamos sin really estar
partidos por la mitad

II
BINATIONAL CABARET
GRINGO CABARET ANIMATEUR VOICE:
ladies & gentlemen
this is the incredible journey
of a 5-year-old Mexican kid
through 4 countries
3 decades
2 languages
& 1 uninterrupted memory
his name is still not clear to me
Guiliermo, Guermo, Yermo, Yiguermo
I believe it means Bill
Bill . . . bill . . . bill . . .
PACHUCO VOICE:

who are you vato loco?
Tantric Charro de las mil y una parrandas
why are you walking down the street
as if you owned this part of the world
this frontera land
so foreign to everyone?

who do you think you are?
Cabeza de Vaca reencarnado?
el primer hipiteca americano, o que?
you wear this new dilemma
like a tattoo in your forehead
but you still don't know what it means
it means, puros chili beans

translation:

NAHUATL VOICE:
yoquimomictilique notatzin ihuan ye yiman on
nomatzin huel omochoquiliaya. Tapan ocalaque
in gringos ihuan zan oquinmocemixohtilique

III
MEMORIES
NORMAL VOICE:
I clearly remember my birth
a major contradiction per se
a mestizo baby born in the Spanish hospital
of a mostly Jewish quarter of Mexico City
right between Virgo & Libra
right in the middle of the decade of the mid-
   century
as the church bells of a wondering San Agustín
were announcing the death of the day
I was being born
from the contradictory lips of Martha
my beautiful mother
who worked in a Kodak shop at the time
primer cuadro:
VOICE WITH MEGAPHONE:
Mexico-Tenochtitlán, 1992

2000 years of dreaming
500 years of nightmare
action!
[*I cover my face with fabric.*]
NASAL VOICE:
the medicine man is brought to trial for
    execution
miento
the Mexican activist is brought to trial for
    deportation
[*I speak in tongues.*]
DRAMATIC VOICE [*pausingly*]:
dear Spanish Inquisition
dear Border Patrol
dear U.S. art world
for 500 years, we've been invisible to you
tu, vous, se, sabe, ve, nada
for 500 years we've been . . . remembering
recordar, desandar, performear
reinventar crímenes contra el Estado
contra uno mismo . . .
[*I freeze for ten seconds.*]
I remember the distorted reflection of my face
in the metal torso of a Spanish soldier named
    Rodrigo
I remember the corpse of a viceroy
in a window display at the financial district
    of Madrid
I remember each & every war
& movement of independence
from the Mayan jungles to the farmlands of
    Wisconsin
I remember Hatuey, Canek & Reies Tijerina
I remember the day Zapata & Villa entered
    "la capital"
blessed with an almost mystical naivete
Zapata, performed by Brando
& Villa, by Telly Savalas
the same day my father brought home the
    first TV
I remember Batman, Mr. Ed & Jungle Jim

the first Americans I ever met
[*I imitate Donald Duck.*]
PACHUCO VOICE:
"Americans que wieerrddd!" I thought
NORMAL VOICE:
I remember drinking out of political sadness
lost between Mexico, Spain & Gringolandia
[*I drink from the shampoo bottle.*]
DRUNKEN VOICE:
I remember cowboy films dubbed in Spain
that memorable scene where John Wayne enters
    the cantina
to find his sweetheart on the lap of a Mexican
    bandito myself
"coño, habeis bebido demasiado" he exclaimed
as I remembered other things
in English & Spanish
English for prose, Spanish for poetry
English for the present, Spanish for the past
English for you, Spanish for us
blackout! Coño!!
[*Blackout*]

IV
aka the Transient Generation
VOICE WITH MEGAPHONE:
un, dos, tres, probando, probando
improvisando en Inglés, Spanglish, Gringoñol
is it clear what I'm talking about?
or do I need to give you more clues?
¡apunten!
NASAL VOICE:
early September, 1988
at the legendary Centro Cultural de la Raza
Supermojado welcomes Superbarrio to the
    grand border wrestling arena
Chicanosaurio and Transvestite Pachuco dance
    a sweaty lambada stage left
Migrasferatu stalks
& the Mexican consul
watches the performance anonadado

CHANTING VOICE:

[*I bark.*]

soy hijo de la crísis fronteriza

soy hijo de la bruja hermafrodita

producto de una cultural cesarean

punkraca heavy mierda all the way

el chuco funkahuatl desertor de 2 paises

vengo del sur

el único de 10 que se pintó

nací entre épocas y culturas y viceversa

nací de una herida infectada

herida en llamas

herida que auuulla

[*I howl.*]

RAPPING VOICE:

soy

porque somos

we are

un fuckin' chingo

the transient generation acá

[*I pause.*]

los high-tech Aztec Raspa Locos Anónimos

for all we have left is dates

places, borders, wounds

all we have left is the hope

to die before the earth

& the will to continue cruisin'

under the Big, Big Smoke

under the Big, Big Smoke

under the Big, Big Smoke

[*I make a sign of the cross while praying.*]

NORMAL VOICE:

norte, sur, este, oeste

Europa, Africa, Asia o América

MEROLICO VOICE:

pos where are we?

West of what?

North of what?

are we migrating in reverse?

or are we simply collecting data for future
    projects?

verbigratia:

NASAL VOICE:

September 23, 1989, Pueblo Colorado

just finished performing at the adobe fort

I drink mezcal with a group of local activists

they want to know everything about my life

NORMAL VOICE:

I remember early trips to Tepoztlan, Havana &
    San Francisco

early dreams about Nirvana & La Chingada

early caresses lost in German skin

hotel rooms, forbidden books & 2nd-hand buses

conversations with Chamula Indians & burned-
    out Europeans

conversations about the true dimensions of the
    world

from metros to miles

every day a bigger world

I used to whisper into the mirror

but one day

the U.S. invaded Grenada

& I realized how small the world was

& how insignificant my vision

[*I perform a shampoo commercial in tongues.
Blackout*]

V

TRANSCULTURAL LOVE

PACHUCO VOICE:

Gran Vato says:

"take an airplane & cry for a vision

but remember güerita,

don't forget to bring your Pepto Bismol

ajuuaaa!"

NASAL VOICE:

summer of '75, somewhere in colorful
    Tacolandia,

a tall American woman looks at me intensely

as if trying to locate me in her past

I grab her by the waist

DRUNKEN VOICE:

remember me?
I used to be . . . I used to be . . . I used to be . . .
was I the chilango hipster you desired so badly
while drinking Kahlua con milk
in the Tacuba Cafe?
or was it at the lobby of the Acapulco Hilton?
I believe you asked
"hey muchiachio, sabis dondi la pot?"
you also said something like
"yo ya tengou machiou parra tonight
pero you ser easy to persuade de lo contrarrío"
LATIN-LOVER VOICE:
you made a fool of yourself in a foreign country
but I didn't mind
pre-semantic communication
was fun & fruitful
remember?
the crux of transcultural love
but everything falls apart
when you finally learn to translate
or when a full house is watching you attentively
MEROLICO VOICE:
por fortuna, aún tenemos
la triple ventaja del lenguaje
para ocultar, conspirar y atacar
verbigratia:
VOICE WITH MEGAPHONE:
ciudadano del mentado primer mundo:
today the roles seem to have reversed
You are a foreigner in your own land
& I am a citizen of this time & place
FAKE SENSITIVE VOICE:
but who do I think I am?
Cuauhtemoc posmoderno
resisting the Hispanic invaders?
a mariachi prophet in Gringolandia?
no, a post-Mexican suffused in ranchero
    nostalgia
no, an angry Chicano lost in the U.S. art world
protagonizing America's capital crisis
its endemic inability to deal with otherness

your endemic inability to deal with me
[*I get shot.*]

VI

MEMORIES
[*I domesticate a rattlesnake in the altar.*]
NASAL VOICE:
early January, 1990
San Ysidro Border checkpoint
I wait in secondary inspection
the guard is furious
'cause I answered him in Spanish
"no señor, no traigo nada
que usted sea capaz de reconocer"
he revises the computer black list
looking for mistakes in my life
I get sad & begin remembering
VOICE WITH THICK MEXICAN ACCENT:
I remember the golden days of Cocoteros
the weekly family dinners
3 generations scanning the past
from Andalucia to Yucatán
from Chihuahua to la capital
ahh, what a permanent world it was
what exquisite food
& all encompassing love
my gentle father leading the toast
to celebrate every inch of the present
[*I pause.*]
& then came the disaster
Cortés arrived in Tenochtitlan
under a cloud of germs
& we began migrating North
amidst earthquakes & fires
from Michoacan to Michigan
across the mirror como quién dice
from Mexico City to San Pancho
across the mirror como quién dice
across the river como quién llora
GRINGOÑOL VOICE:
Tijuana, Juárez, Los Angeles, San Antonio . . .

"1992: A PERFORMANCE CHRONICLE OF THE RE-DISCOVERY OF AMERICA" (first part of a trilogy) The Warrior for Gringostroika addresses his perplexed congregation at The Space, Boston, 1990.

MEROLICO VOICE:
la migra, el miedo, la muerte, ¡la chingada
loooootería!
NORMAL VOICE:
September 1st, 1978. Mexico City airport
Colonial Death Space
my best friends & relatives are gathered to say
good-bye
con mariachis y toda la cosa
I'm going to California, el otro México
& I don't know when I'll be back
as I cross the magnetic checkpoint
I turn & say to them:
"pretendan que estoy a punto de morirme"
"I beg you to pretend I'm about to die
this way you'll get used to my absence"
ausencia, nostalgia, imágen pura . . .
I turn on my inner VCR . . .
[Blackout]

VII
Hypnosis

[I commit hara-kiri in front of a TV monitor.]
NASAL VOICE:
a Chicano performance hypnotist
sneaks through my fractured self
colonizing my fragile Mexican psyche
SLEAZY HARE KRISHNA VOICE [singing]:
Hare Krishna, Krishnahuátl
Hare Nalga, Hairy Nalga
everybody!!
[I freeze for ten seconds.]
HYPNOTIST VOICE:
ommmm . . . rrrelaxxx
[I sign mocos (offensive sign language).]
fall asleep on the map
now walk toward L.A
el lay que nunca vino
shift direction toward Vegas
walk cross-country
cross-language to Miami

visit Nuevo Orleans, Chicago
Detroit, Toronto, Montreal
not one English word
now, face the Northwest
& proceed to walk toward Alaska
& through the Aleutian Chain
into the USSR
in search of the older origins . . .
[I imitate a neanderthal.]
EXHAUSTED VOICE:
I woke up exhausted on stage
not knowing exactly where I was
what a beautiful paradox—I thought
the first Americans came from Russia
40,000 years ago
what brave "illegal aliens"
who dared to cross the border of ice
they walked all the way down
to the Valley of Anáhuac
all the way down
to the bottom of my psyche
NORMAL VOICE:
I remember crossing the Guatemalan border
  in '69
being told by a soldier: "pague o muera"
I remember crossing the U.S. border for the
  first time
I remember being asked to promise to
  never work
I also remember thinking, wait
there's something similar between Guatemala
  & California
there's no people on the streets after 5
at least Guatemalans know they aren't free
at least my audience knows I am not lying

Juliana told me this morning:
"Guillermo, you tend to idealize the South
you also tend to equate the past with the South"
but tell me dear Juliana,

my Brooklyn Yemaya
don't most dreams come from the South?
"false"—she answered
"the dream of America came from the West
Columbus made an unforgivable mistake
& you are following in his footsteps"
[*I pause.*]
"¿porque?"
"he didn't know he had arrived in the
    New World
& neither do you"
[*Blackout*]

VIII
RITOS NECESARIOS
[*I point my finger at an audience member.*]
NORMAL VOICE:
you are here in spite of my will
I am here in spite of yours
we are all here reenacting a historical damnation
la conquista y liberación del Nuevo Mundo
first scene, take two, rolling
NASAL VOICE:
Arlington Texas, 1987
I roam around the stage dressed as
the Arawak slave brought to the Spanish Court
by Christopher Columbus
the first American to ever set foot in Europe
he was left on display for 2 years
until he died of sadness.
my makeup is running down
my audience is 90% redneck
DRUNKEN VOICE:
damas y caballeros
let's stop the performance for a moment
& remember the words of Border Brujo:
a text you probably have already read:
"you are a victim of your government
& so am I . . . of yours
I am here 'cause your government

went down there
to my country
without a formal invitation
& took all our resources
so I came to look for them
nothing else"
has anyone seen my stolen resources?
has anyone seen my coffee,
my gold, my banana, my gas.
my cocaine, my dignity, my wrestling mask?
my ma-ma, ma-ma-cita . . . mamita!! ¿dónde
    andas?
DEVOTIONAL VOICE [*chanting, and with
open arms*]:
holy mother of crises
santos sean tus senos
holy mother of random nostalgia
santas sean tus trenzas
holy mother of the first bus ride
santas sean tus piernas
holy mother of sexual awakening
santas sean tus nalgas
y santa, tu vagina espinada
holy mother of political activism
santa sea tu espalda
holy mother of the departure
santa sea tu memoria
y santos tus tennis shoes
NORMAL VOICE:
I drink from a candle
& dive into my next words
Este, Oeste
politica y sexualidad
NASAL VOICE:
when Cortés met La Malinche
he was shocked by the anger of her beauty
and the clarity of her gestures
he was unable to reconcile
his fear & his passion for her
what a pinche coward el capitán

barbas blancas entre piernas indígenas
beep, beep, beep, caput
communication breakdown . . .
TENDER VOICE:
October 12, 1990
somewhere in this continent
I write on the breasts of my lover:
queridísima C:
I come back to your arms
to remember in your arms
is an act of political defiance
you are guiding me back to the center
    once more
Cocoteros 110, Colonia Nueva Santa María
a 6 kilómetros del Centro Histórico

[*I pause.*]

but wait,
is it possible to ever go back?
I wonder who's trapped in the spiderweb of
    the other?
& where exactly are we?
Havana, Manhattan, Tijuana, Berlin
all axes are breaking my dear,
all borders are fading away
a new decade
demands another cartography
& your kisses are giving me the strength to
    continue
this epic performance-pilgrimage of reconquista

to the end of the North
to the end of the century
to the end of the art world

I faint in her arms
& wake up 3 hours later in Manhattan
scary, peludo, inconmensurable . . .
[*Blackout*]

IX
POST-COLUMBIAN VERTIGO
NASAL VOICE:
I'm entering Manhattan on the L train
surrounded by people from every possible
    nationality
Russians, Filipinos, Africans, Texans, Mixtecos
illegal hybrids of sorts
I feel at home in a world so crowded & eccentric
I call it the end-of-the-century society
I experience a post-Columbian vertigo
[*I speak in tongues (spiced with words such as IBM,
Macintosh, McDonalds, etc).*]
VOICE OF PINTO (prisoner):
I woke up in jail one night
the guard said he'd found me wounded on
    the beach
I saw this mirror dripping blood
& through it
I saw myself dripping blood
from the wounds of my childhood
I had been shaved by the cops
I looked so pitiful
that I decided to hide in my memory
& once again
I was here
there
in the U.S.A.
looking for something I knew didn't exist
the Mexican Weltschmerz
a Hollywood gig
a Sony Walkman
you name it
I was still a tourist
not quite an immigrant yet
not quite a performance artist

I became an immigrant
the day I was forbidden to remember
[*I speak in tongues.*]

los españoles no nos permitieron recordar
the French didn't allow us to remember
the Americans still don't want us to remember
VOICE WITH MEGAPHONE:
Cortés, Maximilian, Emperor Bush
why are you so scared of the past?
[*I pause.*]
hellow, helloow!
are you still there?
can we continue the rehearsal?
testing, testing . . .
dear involuntary cast
imagine this scenario for a film:
FAST-TALKING VOICE:
Queen Isabella is an impresario of the European
common market
a friend of Violeta Chamorro & Salinas de
    Gortari
Columbus is an illegal alien lost in Ohio
Cortés y La Malinche are two transvestites from
    Veracrúz
who migrated to Tijuana
they work in a bar called "La Conquista"
Moctezuma is a ranchero singer dying of AIDS
& Cuauhtémoc, a performance artist from East
    Los Angeles
New Spain now encompasses the old
    territories of
Guatemala, México & the United States of
    Aztlán
the Tortilla Curtain no longer exists
Spanglish has become the official language
Puerto Rico, Hawaii & Panama have finally
    seceded
from the new Federation of U.S. Republics
and a Free Art Agreement has replaced the
Brady Plan
it's marvelous,
wherever we go
we witness the effects of Gringostroika

[*I pause.*]
any reaction?

do you think this film will ever be shot?
cameras rolling . . .
first scene, take one, without subtitles

X

NOCHE DE SORPRESAS Y AFICIONADOS
CABARET ANIMATEUR VOICE:
Los Angeles, 1992
noche de sorpresas y aficionados
en el bar "La Gloria Tecno-Azteca"
damas y caballeros, quiet please
tonight we are proud to present
an authentic 3rd World performance saga
low-tech but filled with love, magic & violence
written, directed & performed
by "El Charromántico"
acompañado por sus 12 naked mariachis
un aplauso por favor . . .¡
VOICE OF EL PIPORRO (famous Mexican
singer):
thank you, thank you
this song is dedicated to all of you out there
beautiful razzza
undiscovered aborígenas
para ustedes, "El Rey del Cruce . . ."
[*I sing.*]
"una yerba en el camino
me enseño que mi destino
era cruzar y cruzar

por ahí me dijo un troquero
que no hay que cruzar primero
pero hay que saber cruzar

con tarjeta o sin tarjeta
digo yo la pura neta
y mi palabra es la ley . . .

no tengo troca ni jaina
ni raza que me respalda
pero sigo siendo de L.A."
DRUNKEN VOICE:
you only know how lonely you are
when you stand in front of so many lonely
    people
[*I pause.*]
shit! this part belongs to another script
but, where the hell is that other script?
stop that pinche cámara!!
[*I signal an invisible TV camera operator.*]
now, press the rewind button . . . stop!
NASAL VOICE:
as I was saying
La Esperanza bar closed at midnight
I hit the streets of Tijuana
along with a gang of Marines
they were speaking an incomprehensible dialect
something like . . .
[*I snap my fingers as if looking for an idea, then
speak English bicameral interwoven with words like
"fuck" and "dollars."*]
I believe they were talking about
how much they hated women, Mexicans &
    communists
[*Blackout*]

XI
MORE MEMORIES
[*I put on the Indian headdress.*]
NORMAL VOICE:
I remember living at the intersection of 20
    mythologies
PIPORRO VOICE:
I remember the cowboys at the Saugus Cafe
who insisted on buying me drinks
'cause they thought I was an Indian
but made me pay the bill
when they discovered I was Mexican
I remember Mimi, the albino trumpet player

from Alaska
who thought we could become famous as a
    comical duo
"Aztec boy y la trompeta de hielo"
I remember the punk parties at Jaimie X
I remember thinking that by slam-dancing
I could exorcise my pre-Columbian pathos
I remember 6 ribs broken by cultural clash
[*I scream.*]
ay!, ay!, ay!, ay!, ay!
NAHUATL VOICE:
amo otlacualoc oncan techtlanahualiz quename
ye huitz atlatlacamamaniliztli.
amo otimatiaya hueyi quahuitl ihuan de
    tlacatecolotl

XII
ONE OF MANY DEPARTURES
NORMAL VOICE:
parto, luego existo
one can only exorcise this pathos by departing
NASAL VOICE:
it's January 1st, 1988
my 64th trip to the U.S.A.
'scaping the Spanish Inquisition
little did I know
they had offices in Gringolandia
I travel on a train full of high-spirited migrant
    workers
I turn on my inner radio:
[*I sing.*]
yo no soy un mojado sin visa
ni tampoco un vil exiliado
yo lo único que quiero
is to come to the North
y que me dejen vacilar sin ton sin son
VOICE OF MELANCHOLIC RAPPER:
a long & lonely road to the most dangerous
    place on earth
Califas, home of La Reina de Los Angeles
a long & dangerous journey to her arms

a melancholic journey to the center of the
    art world
it's all behind me
35 years of life at the end of
5 centuries of death
global crises, border dreams
time to find a new language
and a brand-new performance jacket
[*I pause.*]
time to change the location so to speak
DRUNKEN VOICE:
where chingados are we?
I'm sinking, sinking
in the turquoise waters of the Caribbean
1/2 a mile from Isla Mujeres
I'm clearly young & fucked up
& my friends are busy
seducing a group of French anthopologists
    ashore
VOICE WITH FRENCH ACCENT:
are you authentic Mayan or Mixteco?
are you a poet or an actor?
ÑERO VOICE:
guatever yu want señorita
[*Blackout*]

XIII
Street Performance
[*I light a toke, put on the bandana, take off my
jacket, and open my arms.*]
NORMAL VOICE:
Los Angeles again, Spring of '91
I sit on the sidewalk naked
my political arms are exhausted
dozens of slogans are written all over my body
I quote:
[*I snap my fingers with each quote.*]
"to perform is to return"
"to arrive is just an illusion"
"the map is catching on fire"
"California fornicare sin memoria"

"chinga tu Mare Nostrum"
"Spanglish, the language of the future"
"censorship, the opposite of glasnost"
& many others frankly illegible to you
people begin to gather around me
I look at them with demonic tenderness
I finally exclaim:
VOICE OF PINTO (prisoner):
"the other is thinking of you
I am the other
but you might no longer be yourself"
REDNECK VOICE:
"speak from the heart, not from the script!!"
NORMAL VOICE:
someone yells, a plant perhaps
"the script is my very heart," I answer
each line, a vein that links 2 arteries
a line that divides 2 countries
a nail that scratches your retina
coma
estado de coma global
identidad descuartizada
VOICE WITH MEGAPHONE:
the East/West border collapses
the North/South border is militarized
you are forcing me to rethink the entire
    performance
forcing me to cross the border once more
[*Blackout*]

XIV
Border Blaster
MEROLICO DJ VOICE:
Laredo, Piedras Negras, Pilsen, Echo Park,
pos where are we?
West of what?
North of what?
Arteamérica
tierra de convictos y alucinados
acá
su servidor el Charrollero

la lengua más veloz de la frontera
broadcasting from border blaster WXYZ
    Tijuana
good evening ladies & germs
I would like to dedicate this chorizo
to all the pluribus raza
who have risked their fundillos
for the creation of a New World Border
digo, el maextro Gordochev, el cojonudo de
    Mandela
Vaclav Havel, Daniel "el chili" Ortega, el padre
    Aristide
Arafat, Superbarrio, Fray Tormenta, "el
    Icuiricui" . . .
pa' todos ellos con afecto y admiración
este danzón de fin de siglo
[*I freeze for ten seconds.*]
RADIO ANNOUNCER VOICE:
Radio Fin de Siglo
1990 megahertz en todas direcciones
RADIO EVANGELIST VOICE:
dear Tribe of the Inflamed Eyelids:
wherever you may be
in Baghdad, Berlin or Panama
are you listening to my holy words?
I wonder who will outlive this crisis?
who will walk safely across the bridge of the
    century?
& who will be left to listen
to the birth screams of the next millennium?
[*I howl. Blackout*]

XV
TERRA IGNOTA
NORMAL VOICE:
terra ignota . . . sin mota
2 miles before the end of the North
I get very sentimental
I write a bunch of postcards:
MELANCHOLIC VOICE:
dear father

I promise I'll hold the family together
dear mother
I promise I'll wear my father's clothes
dear Alfredo
I promise I will take you to the U.S. on my back
dear Gui, my only son
I promise I will teach you survival skills in
    Spanish
dear granma
I promise I'll stay strong
for at least another decade
for at least another performance
dear audience
I promise I will try to piece myself together
dear Juliana
I promise I will finish this performance
one of these days
& you & I will descend to the temazcalli
with my son and best friends
we will sweat our angst away
& co-imagine better options for the future
GRAVE VOICE:
el gran performance pilgrimage
toward the North of the future
across the U.S.A. border
across my Mexican memory
la memoria de la lengua
or what's left of it
NORMAL VOICE:
I remember burning the 3 caravels of Columbus
on the shores of Imperial Beach
I remember Tijuacóatl spitting fire across the
    border fence
20 artistas busted for disrupting the binational
    order
I remember harassing the Canadian border
    patrol
with this very megaphone
from the other shore of the Niagara river
VOICE WITH MEGAPHONE:
nationality?

sexual preference?
got any papers? . . . to roll, I mean
NORMAL VOICE:
I remember Border Brujo myself
performing with torches
at the Adobe Fort of Pueblo Colorado
& then at the Teatro del Estado de Mexicali
at the Convention Center of Vladivostok
at the Brooklyn Academy of Music
at a migrant-worker center of Southern Florida
At a Cinco de Mayo parade in Santa Monica
& so on & so forth
until the brujo died of exhaustion
& I was born from the ashes of his last word
his last word was . . .
[*I freeze.*]
PACHUCO RAPPER VOICE
[*moving hands softly*]:
did I ever melt?
did I ever arrive?
did I lose enough of myself in the bloody
    crossing?
am I the same stubborn 15-year-old chilango
snake boots & rockabilly toupée
ever looking for trouble & truth
in the most dangerous corners of the city?
a city which no longer exists
Tenochtitlan
10 years after the conquest
Mexico D.F.
6 years after the quake
San Francisco de Asismo
9 years after the plague
stop!
stop I say!!
[*I scream at the light technicians.*]
can't you guys do something more creative with
    the lights?
I mean, this is a real crucial moment in the piece!
Columbus is just about to land & shit!!
[*Lights go crazy.*]

NORMAL VOICE:
fine, fine, don't overdo it 'cause
I'm looking for a dangerous place
I'm looking for a dangerous phrase
something like . . .
[*I hesitate, then I snap my fingers.*]
"when you forget what's next
you step in the wound by accident"
[*I get very excited.*]
so here I go, my accidental friends . . .
NASAL VOICE:
October 12, 1992
Ellis Island, New York
the tribe & I are about to land
on a low-rider carabela
a huge banner reads
"500 años de genocidio"
y aquí andamos todavía vida mía
[*I stand up and adopt a heroic Columbus-like
stance.*]
MEROLICO VOICE WITH MEGAPHONE:
hellow America!
soy Cristóbal Cogelón, el otro man
unofficial performance chronicler de la Nueva
Santa María
alias "El Warrior de la Gringostroika"
& I just . . .
discovered you . . . discovered you [*in loop*]
[*I point at an audience member.*]
therefore you exist
per omnia saecula speculorum
con saffoosss . . .
[*I perform offensive Mexican sign language.
Blackout*]

XVI
ADMIRAL OF THE OCEAN SEA
VOICE WITH MEGAPHONE:
5 centuries
4 races
3 languages

2 faces
1 heart
action:
the night before the awaited arrival
the Admiral of the Ocean Sea
confronts his restless crew:
PACHUCO VOICE:
no se asusten carnales
It's only me, the transatlantic vato
& I've got some questions for you
are you a citizen of this time & place
or are you still clinging to a dying order?
are you willing to dialogue?
or are you going to shoot me after the show?
are you ready to co-write with me the
    next chapter?

XVII
ARS FRONTÉRICA
NORMAL VOICE:
Matachín,
remember only what you want
the rest is poisonous algae
toxic waste in your mental tundra
lingüo lae ars frontérica
[*I speak in tongues.*]
I remember speaking in tongues since I was 12
always wondering if I was mad or enlightened
either or
I remember things in English or in Spanish
English for politics, Spanish for love
English for praxis, Spanish for theory
English for survival, Spanish for laughter
English for time, Spanish for space
English for art, Spanish for literature
lingüo lae ars frontérica
[*I imitate Donald Duck.*]
NORTEÑO VOICE:
have I finally lost my accent?
MEROLICO VOICE:
have I finally lost my accent?

GRINGOÑOL VOICE:
have I finally lost my accent?
you no entender un carrayo perro sounds
    mucho interesting
[*I bark.*]
NASAL VOICE:
Tenochtitlan, 1512
Spanish becomes the "official language" of
    Nova Hispania
miento:
San Diego, 1988
English becomes the "official language" of
    the Southwest
Mezkin performance artist Charrollero
addresses a group of quote unquote
"Latinou gang members & ex-pintos"
DIDACTIC VOICE:
repeat with me:
"censura no es cultura"
"a la chingada el Inglés Oficial"
"fuck Official English" 'cause . . .
PACHUCO VOICE:
I speak Spanglish 'cause reality is broken
I speak wierd shit 'cause times are weird
    ¿que no?
I stutter 'cause I'm about to die, about to die
in front of your very eyes, your very eyes
I'm dying
as a Mexican is dying
& a Chicano is being born
[*I open my legs and push as if giving birth.*]
I'm giving birth
to the new passenger in my body
Part II of this performance saga
parto luego existo
[*I sing.*]
"adios pampa mia, me voy a tierras lejanas . . ."
VOICE WITH ARGENTINE ACCENT:
adiós Guillermo III, capitán de barco hundido
adiós Comanche Pinto, guerrero de
    experimentos marginales

adiós Super-mojado, samurai de cruces
    cumbancheros
adiós muchachos compañeros de la huída
adiós país de promesas desmembradas
adios me muero, regreso y me volteo
hacia mi nueva corteza ontológica
MEXICO CITY ÑERO VOICE:
ontológica?
¿on toy, lógica? ¿on tamos?
y con la mismisima capa del tinieblas
el más chido luchador
catapulto mis poemas hacia el norte
norteño soy, norteado voy y bien mojado
Cristobal Culón "el indiocumentado"
el mero mero y voy que vuelo
sin brújula ni caravela
al otro lado del infierno
VOICE OF AUTHORITY WITH MEGA-
PHONE [*pausing between questions*]:
alo?
did you ever arrive?
were you able to jump over the fence?
could you step into the mirror
without cutting yourself?
without slashing your epidermic dignity?
did you make it to the new decade?
in time to participate in the change
or did you witness it from a distance?
hello?, hello?!
can you still hear me?
or have you already departed
to another land, another language, another
    text . . .
[*Blackout*]

XVIII
SPANISH LESSON
NORMAL VOICE:
"there is a distance between us
that reminds me of who I am
néhuatl nimopo

néhuatl oic onimitzcocolli"
says Cuauhtémoc to Cortés
while being tortured
[*I pause.*]
más lo cortés no quita lo culero
Spanish lesson #1
ÑERO VOICE:
culero es aquel
que conociendo dos o más lenguajes
solo te muestra uno
GRINGOÑOL VOICE:
translation:
culeirou is someone who speaks
two or more languages
but always answers in the one you don't know
Bush tambíen ezz un culeirou
blackout!!
[*Blackout*]

XIX
MORE MEMORIES
NASAL VOICE:
Times Square, New York City
an electronic billboard reads:
"today you have 2 choices in America:
contribute to Gringostroika
or let nostalgia drive you bananas"
verbigratia:
[*I stand up and howl.*]
I remember yodeling in the Alps with a group of
    Swiss campesinos
howling in the Rockies with my immigrant
    friends
drunk out of our minds & our countries
I remember dancing salsa in the mountains of
    North Carolina
with a bunch of Southern artists
dancing yuyu in a London bar
with a bunch of Rasta blonds
I remember not knowing where I was anymore
inside or outside myself

fiction or social reality
EVANGELIST VOICE:
the borders were drifting away
the map was catching on fire
weather changes in every place of your psyche
rowdy winds demolishing your fragile identity
"¡auxilio!" you said in perfect Spanish
but no one was there to rescue you
cue, cue, cue . . .
[*I speak to the technicians.*]
cue the fuckin' tape maestro!
VOICE WITH MEGAPHONE:
everybody quiet!
[*I pause.*]
the show begins for the 2nd time
la 3a es la vencida
action:
Gómez-Peña as a performer of cultural mistakes
[*I put on the hat or the mask.*]
NORMAL VOICE:
I remember my first appointments
with the guardians of cultural
    misunderstanding:
I remember being thrown out of a deli
'cause I said I wanted a kidnap instead of a
    napkin
I remember being sent to secondary inspection
'cause I told a humorless border guard
I had an appointment with freedom
I remember each of the 7 times
the California police busted me for "looking
    suspicious"
for "looking Iranian"
for "looking exactly like the dealer they were
    after"
for "stealing my radio"
for wearing a wrestler mask on the 4th of July
for walking at night in a country
that has forbidden darkness
I'm glad I'm able to remember these moments
& share them with you as art

with all my love & all my anger
BREATHY VOICE:
ay, my Southern affection
my border nostalgia
my Northern wrath
la vida loca
la vida en llamas
placazo de la memoria
[*I freeze.*]
FROM NORMAL TO MEROLICO VOICES:
I choose to continue remembering
the singular journey
that led me to this stage
5 centuries of foreign domination
total
492 performances
in which
I've cut my hair
sliced my wrists
farted & eaten on stage
danced on fire & ice
recreated my birth
invoked my ancestors
conspired against the government
asked for a job
sold my identity
deported myself back to Mexico
repositioned my soul within my body
reshaped my body to accommodate your whims
or to confirm your fears
aquí, tu miedo encarnado
en mi cuerpo
[*I stand up and begin to march.*]
MILITARY CHANTING VOICE:
my body elastic
mi cuerpo celluloid
my body pasional
mi cuerpo folcloric
my body cartographic
mi cuerpo cyber-punk
my body rupestre

mi cuerpo ceremonial
my body militant
mi cuerpo metaphor
my bloody body
cuerpo adentro
me interno
en un concierto
de adioses
me amortajo
hacia el futuro incierto
adiós, adiós
década del pánico
siglo del progreso
milenio de la guerra
arte occidental
arte marginal . . .
[*I click my boots and perform fascist salute.*]
AUTHORITARIAN VOICE:
¡América!
I say América-ca-ca-ca
VOICE WITH MEGAPHONE:
welcome to the great international community
here, no one understands you
here, no one wants to be like you
here, you are just another country
with big weapons and small aspirations
it's 1991 & the dream is almost over
for CNN, Charrollero servidor
disapproved by military censors
[*I speak in tongues. Blackout*]

XX
DEATH PRAYER
NASAL VOICE:
Christmas night
at the temple of the Basílica de Guadalupe
in Mexico City
my family & I are wearing all black
my nephew Ricardiaco listens to Jello Biafra on
    his Walkman
the priest speaks of the bleeding memories of

Mexico
his voice overlaps with mine
I begin to remember so many memorable deaths
throughout my years
documented deaths/undocumented years:
OLD WOMAN'S VOICE:
Cuauhtémoc, Canek, Guevara
Neruda, Rosario Castellanos, Althusser
Fassbinder, Cortázar, Roque Dalton
Allende, José Alfredo Jiménez, Indira Gandhi
Abbie Hoffman, Joseph Beuys, Ana Mendieta
my father, Sid Vicious, Pedro Vargas . . .
"more men than women die
women are always stronger"
NORMAL VOICE:
said Granpa Carlos while dying in Spanish
I certainly expect to die
before my compañera
especulando, especulando
how could I witness without her
the grand eclipse of the century?
how could I face the Great Rupture
without my other half?
[*Blackout*]

XXI
FRAGMENTOS
NASAL VOICE:
Stanford University
I stand in front of an academic audience
linguists, sociologists, anthropologists
surveilling my "authenticity" los muy cabrones
MEROLICO & PACHUCO VOICES
[*alternating*]:
me dicen el half & half
half-Indian/half-Spaniard
half-Mexican/half-Chicano
half-son/half-father
half-artist/half-writer
half-wolf/half-eagle
half-always/half-never

[*I look for someone in the audience.*]
ROMANTIC VOICE:
& you my dear C
will you dare to love
such an incomplete creature?
the Spaniards, the gringos & the art world
left me all fractured & angry
lenguas muertas para oídos muertos
[*I perform jitanjáforas and sound poems in
crescendo. I cover myself with an Indian cloth.*]
GRINGO VOICE:
does he speak in Aztecou, Esperanto or
    Cholo-punk?
is he a terrorist, a brujo or a performance artist?
is he being harrassed by Cortés or the Border
    Patrol?
ANGRY VOICE:
¡¡confiesa hijo de la. . . !!
¡¡ay!!
¡¡confiesa hijo de la. . . !!
¡¡ay!!
TIRED VOICE [*pausingly*]:
mouth is dry
liver is weak
veins are swollen
haven't slept in 12 years
haven't stopped walking since I left
haven't arrived to the North of my dream
I'm not even sure there is a North really
not even sure I really exist
do I?
do I?
do I?
I see my face on the page
but I hardly recognize it
[*I put on blond wig.*]
GRINGO VOICE:
"kill the stereotype!" you said . . .
NORMAL VOICE:
stereotype?
estereotipo #39

a 3rd-class citizen in a First World country
the Mexican as flamboyant victim of cultural
    misunderstanding
[*I begin pulling the wig down slowly.*]
TRANSVESTITE VOICE:
one night I was beaten up by a biker gang from
    Hollywood
one of my first leading roles in an American
    thriller
they mistook me for a Columbian dealer
a Filipino boxer, a Libyan Pachuco, a Hawaiian
    surfer
who knows what they thought they knew
I've been mistaken so many times in America
[*I pause.*]
but then, who hasn't?
people here tend to mistake each other's j118
identities
it's like a national sport
GRINGO VOICE:
are you Peruvian or Venezuelan?
were you speaking Mexican or Spanish?
did I see you on the TV of my fears?
NASAL VOICE:
when Columbus arrived in Las Américas
he was convinced he had found a shortcut to the
    Indies
the very discovery of this continent was a flat
    misunderstanding
& let's not forget that misunderstanding is the
    seed of all violence
cambio:
when President Bush arrived in the Persian Gulf
he was convinced he had found a shortcut to the
    New World Order
but his interpretation of Islam was a flat
    misunderstanding
& let's not forget that misunderstanding is the
seed of all
violence
[*Blackout*]

XXII
BINATIONAL PERFORMANCE
NORMAL VOICE:
angry mob in the background
an insurrection in my mind
& a bunch of German tourists
recording my voice with a nagra
testing, testing . . .
1,2,3, testing . . .
testing the IQ of my audience
the Warrior for Gringostroika takes over my
tongue
PACHUCO VOICE WITH MEGAPHONE:
helloww rrazzza . . .
can you hear me?
I'm standing right on the U.S./Mexico
    borderline
with a foot on each country siii . . .
the line is actually bisecting my manhood
got a Mexican huevo
& an American ball
& on top of that
I've got a poem for you
check it out:
[*I unzip my pants and pull a poem out from my
crotch. I subvocalize for twenty seconds. Blackout*]

XXIII
PIRATE RADIO
NORMAL VOICE:
flashback:
Radio Berlin, September of 1983
INTERVIEWER VOICE WITH GERMAN
ACCENT:
but Mr. Gómezz
where exactly do you live?
& who are you really?
SOFT RAP VOICE [*while snapping fingers*]:
soy el otro fuera de mí
el otro dentro de tí
the other tras de tí

tu sombra espanticida
your sticky Mexican shadow
y al borde de la border
me inclino
y te reclamo
INTERVIEWER VOICE:
meaning what?
MEROLICO VOICE [*speaking very fast*]:
I live in the other Mexico
injertado en las entrañas del etcétera
the metropolitan area that extends
from Méjico Deefe to San Pancho California
with branches in every major city of the West
including Piedras Negras & Brooklyn
y desde acá XEKK
transmito y me reinvento
voila
INTERVIEWER VOICE:
I don't know what you mean
you Mexicans are flowery & redundant
PACHUCO VOICE [*snapping fingers*]:
I mean
soy "am"
the double other
el 7 masks
el charro-punk
el cholomatic
el Krishnahuátl
& I'm about
to escape once more
from the prison of your perceptions
voilaaaa . . .
cambio de canal
VOICE WITH FRENCH ACCENT:
Ici c'est le Radio Publique Montreal
September 23, 1989
by the way, I just turned 34
INTERVIEWER VOICE WITH FRENCH
ACCENT:
how exactly has your identity been affected
by your experience of Amerique?

VOICE WITH THICK LATINO ACCENT:
to "be" in America, I mean in this America
is a complicated matter
you "are" in relation to the multiplicity of looks
you are able to display
I am brown therefore I'm underdeveloped
I wear a moustache therefore I am Mexican
I gesticulate therefore I'm Latino
I am horny therefore I am a sexist
I speak about politics therefore I'm
    un-American
my art is indescribable therefore I'm a
    performance artist
I talk therefore I am, period.
INTERVIEWER VOICE:
c'est fascinánti
VOICE WITH THICK LATINO ACCENT:
in order to multiply the perceptual readings of
    my identity
I always try to create interference during the
    broadcast
verbigratia
NORMAL VOICE:
San Antonio, Radio Armageddon
RADIO PREACHER [*inflammatory*]:
good evening children of evil
there is a war in the streets of America
in the schools & parks of your neighborhoods
in your very home & workplace
between races & generations
men & women
hippies & punks
cops & "coloreds"
government censors & radical artists
a nasty war is taking place right now
in this very moment
someone out there wishes my words were lies
[*Macabre laughter*]
tonight we have a very distinguished guest
a border warrior, a post-modern Geronimo
a conceptual "wetback" whose life

epitomizes this . . .
[*I continue mouthing, and spread my arms as if
being executed.*]
DRAMATIC VOICE:
nine, ocho, seven, seis, five, cuatro, three, dos
[*Pre-recorded gun shots*]
[*I begin to die in slow motion, then suddenly freeze.*]
SOFT-SPOKEN VOICE:
I dreamt in English that the U.S. had become a
    totalitarian state
controlled by satellites & computers
I dreamt that in this strange society
poets and artists had no public voice whatsoever
thank god it was just a dream
"English only," just a dream
not a memory
Jesse Helms, just a dream
not a memory
my oldest memory being
[*I speak in tongues.*]
NASAL VOICE WITH MEGAPHONE:
we interrupt this radio-novella
to give you an important message:
migrant God Quetzalcóatl is now crossing
the U.S./Mexico border by foot
he's coming once more to give you
the basic secrets of agriculture, education & art
be willing to listen, be willing to . . .
[*Blackout*]

XXIV
Spanglish Lesson
DIDACTIC PACHUCO VOICE:
okay vatos
repeat with me:
vivir en estado de sitio
is a translatable statement
to live in state of siege
es suceptible de traducción
an Aztec in Nova Hispania
a Mexican in San Diego

a Portorrican in New York
a Moroccan in Paris
a Pakistani in London
definitely a translatable condition
PACHUCO VOICE:
vivir en estado de alerta
is also translatable my dear
RAPPING VOICE:
to live in state of alert
with your wings ready to flap
& your eyes ready to question
[*I snap my fingers and scream.*]
why, why, why, why . . .
Ayy!! I, I
a child of the Mexican crisis
a new foreigner in the art world
allowed to exhibit his wounds
in immaculate neon coffins . . .
why, why, why . . .
NEWSCASTER VOICE:
the war goes on in El Salvador
as the performance continues in [*city in which I
am performing*]
sorry
the war goes on in the Persian Gulf
as the performance continues in [*city in which I
am performing*]
same war, different performance
aquí, allá
al Sur . . . de la . . . Chingada
[*Blackout*]

XXV
Memory

NORMAL VOICE:
I remember the cool waters of Veracrúz
where Cortés decided to burn his ships
his point being
there was no way back to the Old World

I remember the cold waters of California

where I decided to burn my tennis shoes
my point being
there was no way back to Mexico

today, 12 years later
I still don't regret it
still haven't finished this text
but God, thy Father Tezcatlipoca
Lord of Border Misconceptions
haven't I spilled blood all over the map?

XXVI
Ad Lib TV

NASAL VOICE:
San Diego, Channel 12
Super-mojado loses his cool
in the middle of a TV interview
the pro-producers are shitting in their pants
DRUNKEN VOICE:
the Spaniards arrived on a Monday
I left my country on a Tuesday
the San Juanico fire occurred on a Wednesday
& the Mexico City earthquake on a Thursday
my father died on a Friday
my son was born on a Saturday
& my best performance ever took place on
    a Sunday
I think . . .
in each of these days,
a bunch of us Mexican wolves
got together to lick each other's tears
'cause you know carnales
this kind of pain is only bearable as ritual
[*I howl or grab candle and drink.*]
& my psyche is the only document left
a performance document
for the end-of-the-century society
[*I light a joint while speaking in tongues.*]
NORMAL VOICE:
recordamos, recordamos, recordamos . . .
we remember, we remember, we remember . . .

we remember dreaming about the arrival
    of Cortés
not knowing exactly what a hairy man on
    a horse was
we thought the Spaniards were gods
& our fate was to welcome them
we still carry the weight of that mistake

we also remember the arrival of the first turista
not knowing exactly what a blond man on a
donkey was
we thought the gringos were gods
& our fate was to welcome them
CABARET ANIMATEUR VOICE:
ladies & gentlemen
it is my fate to welcome you
to my performance continent
música maestro:
[*Music*]
DRUNKEN VOICE:
Europe, welcome to the Third World
Cortés, welcome to Tenochtitlán
Baker, welcome to the source of the Nile
Herzog, welcome to Perú
Gauguin, welcome to Tahiti
Artaud, welcome to Chihuahua
Lowry, welcome to the barranca
Lennon, welcome to Calcutta
you welcome to me
free rum for all of you
[*I show my tongue to a woman in the audience.*]
SEXY VOICE:
hey, babe!
give me a chance & I'll give you my passion
give me a contract & I'll give you my talents
give me a loan & I'll give you my oil
give me a visa & I'll give you my memory . . .
give me a job & I'll give you my language
painful but necessary transactions
we are hungry not horny I mean
[*I make horny noises.*]

I wonder . . .
I wonder when will the cycle break?
a broken record, a broken record
[*I scream.*]
ay, my broken heart!!
[*Blackout*]

XXVII
PIRATE RADIO
PACHUCO DJ VOICE:
hello America
this is the voice of Gran Vato Charrollero
broadcasting from the hot deserts of Nogales,
    Arizona
zona de libre cogercio
2000 megahertz en todas direcciones . . .
today, September 7, of 1989
you are celebrating Labor Day in Seattle
while the Klan demonstrates
against Mexicans in Georgia
ironía, 100% ironía
today, November 20, 1989
your führer has invaded Panama
in search of a bad performance artist
Noriega hides in the Vatican embassy
imagine, qué loquerai
500 years ago
Europe didn't even imagine
this continent existed
500 years ago
this continent was . . .
[*I mouth.*]
DRUNKEN VOICE:
wait, my memory is failing again
are you the cousin of the uncle
of the mother of someone
I can't remember?
or am I making it up
'cause after all
this is just a bad performance
in a country that has forbidden memory?

a country whose name I can't even remember
U.S.A. I think
United States of Am . . . nesia
yes, your government really did a number on me
left me all amnesiac & shit
let's celebrate the death of memory
with a bottle of words
[*I grab the bottle and drink.*]
wait, my memory is coming back
NASAL VOICE:
Los Angeles, 1982
Bishop Misterio addresses his gringo
   congregation:
EPIPHANIC VOICE:
I ask you to join in this communion
[*I take another bottle and drink.*]
this is "Elixir de Pasión"
I drink it every night
to renew my hormones & spice my saliva
would anyone care for a sip?
[*Someone stands up and grabs the bottle. Bishop
Misterio grabs another bottle.*]
this is "saliva de gato" para el miedo
I drink it every morning
it protects me against racism
formalism & reborn christianity
who will dare to drink from it?
[*Someone grabs the bottle. The congregation
laughs.*]
& this is "Elixir de Misterios Ancestrales"
it helps me to remember
drink, drink my children
but just a little sip
or you might grow hair in your $#@&*
pass these bottles around & commune with my
   madness
when I speak we make art together
when I speak we slowly create a new world
[*I freeze. Blackout*]

XXVIII
MORE MEMORIES
NORMAL VOICE:
camara . . . ¡acción!
I remember the day I arrived in California
as if it were yesterday
the lonely Greyhound station of Los Angeles
smelling like hypodermic piss
the 3 undercover cops who welcomed me
with a sudden "no loitering, out!!"
the lack of social & verbal skills of Californians
the gargantuan size of the sandwiches & the
   Marines
the width of the sky; the depth of the faults
the artificial happiness in the faces of the blonds
the endemic anger in the faces of the "others"
that anger seemed to be one of the few real
   things in movieland
PACHUCO VOICE:
scary but real
real pain comanche
deep loneliness maextro
SOFT VOICE:
I remember falling into a trance on stage
I remember the day I came back from the
Flower Wars
Ixtaccíhuatl had turned into ice for me
& I had decided to let myself die
to fulfill the damn prophecy
but instead I parted
left my skin without color
& crossed the border of Anahuac
to regain the desired citizenship
they had so cruelly denied me

but who are they?—you ask me.

XXIX
LETTER
NASAL VOICE:
at the new Taco Bell of San Juan Capistrano

undocumented Christopher Columbus
tired, ill & misunderstood
scribbles a strange letter to Queen Isabella
VOICE WITH SPANISH ACCENT
[*solemnly*]:
Salve Reina de todos los Imperios,
my phony green card states
Resident Alien # 00141932
my last medical exams reveal
high cholesterol & low blood pressure
my bank account is empty
my desire is one day to go back
from Califas to Nova Hispania
and further back
from Salvador Island to Palos
my Ergo Motto reads:
TENDER VOICE:
"to sail the waves of Horror Vacui"
"cruzar el estrecho del Mictlán"
mi Reina de Todas las Aguas
will you wait for me
in the other side of the ocean?
will you wait for me
in the other side of my tongue?
will my voice break into your future dreams?
or will you be dead when I go back?
[*Blackout. I deliver following during blackout.*]
VOICE WITH MEGAPHONE:
dear actors, dancers, musicians, poets
are we ready to start the show?
or should I go back to Mexico?
[*No answer*]
OK, I'm going back!

XXX
PRIVATE RITUAL
[*I appear sitting on a chair with my pants down. I
slowly apply war makeup while delivering the
following.*]
TROUBLED VOICE:

I'm shitting in my Mexico City 100-year-old
    toilet
filled with gases, memories & joy
I re-mem-ber performing Smogman
in my Catholic high school
my first play ever to be seen
by people who didn't really want to
I remember my first performances in the U.S.
wrapped with an Indian cloth in fetal position
left alone for 2 days in a public elevator
I remember bringing my audience to the edge of
    Freeway 5
screaming at the cars to stop & save me from
    shipwreck
I remember burning the best photo of my
    mother
while screaming to the heavens:
"madre, házme regresar a la placenta!"
from high-tech to Aztec . . . via . . . performance
    art
[*I continue to apply makeup while I speak in
tongues.*]
FROM NORMAL TO MEROLICO VOICES:
I speak therefore I continue to be
language, my passport to your country
language, my journey to your arms
language, my most effective weapon
language, my 2-way ticket to the past
language
my abracadabra
a memory per line
a thread of life per sentence
10 dollars a poem
postcard included
life in Gringolandia,
a cheese TV talk show
a color-Xerox photo-novella
10 video lessons on misinformation
stop!
[*Blackout*]

XXXI

FINALE

SOFT VOICE [*slowly*]:
Europe owns no other continent
Eurown discovery not continent
disco-very strange co-
descubrimiento descubro, miento . . .
I lie to you . . .
we don't lie together
in the end
we never lie together
vecinos abismales
still undiscovered
to one another
not quite carnales yet
not quite connecting
NORMAL VOICE:
Border Field Park
2 years after the fall of the Berlin Wall
REPORTER VOICE:
I lie on the beach
waiting for Christopher Columbus

to discover me
for the 500th time

It's October 12, midday
& the cameras are waiting like me
Televisa & CBS are ready to record history
or better said, to re-invent it
the fanfares of Turismo are growing intense
my heart speeds up as my tongue writhes
my tongue goes physically crazy
[*I speak in tongues and jitanjáforas.*]
but this time Columbus didn't arrive
Spain & Italy were so busy
fighting over credits
that the entire production
was postponed til '99

I go back to the city
to think of a better text
to put into practice
thank you, my other selves, my other voices
for traveling with me tonight
[*I blow out the candles.*]

FIN

PERFORMANCE
CHRONOLOGY

1979 "THE LONELINESS OF THE IMMIGRANT" A 24-hour ritual performance at a public elevator, Los Angeles. A text on the wall read: "Moving to another country hurts more than moving to another house, another face, another lover....In one way or another we all are or will be immigrants. Surely one day we will be able to crack this shell open, this unbearable loneliness, and develop a transcontinental identity..."(From the archives of The Broken Line).

1982 "THE THIRD REALITY" Amy Knoles, Gómez-Peña, and Sara-Jo Berman in an early performance of the Poyesis Genética Troupe, Cal Arts, Valencia. (From the archives of Poyesis Genética).

1983 "THE BALLAD OF MISTER MISTERIO AND SALOME" Gómez-Peña and Sara-Jo Berman perform their bilingual mixture of border cabaret and experimental performance art. (From the archives of Poyesis Genética).

1985 "EL SUPER-CHICANO" (BORDER SUPERHERO) Image for the poster/brochure of "Ocnoceni," the last performance of Poyesis Genética. Designed by Gómez-Peña, this image also became a velvet painting and was referenced in various performance texts.

1986 "THE END OF THE LINE" A site-specific performance at the U.S./Mexico border, by the Border Arts Workshop. Documentary scenes of this performance can be seen in the film *Mi Otro Yo/My Other Self*, directed by Philip and Amy Brookman.(From the BAW-TAF archives).

1987 "GENERIC LATIN AMERICAN DICTATOR IN EXILE IN LA JOLLA"   From the series "Documented/Indocumentado." A collaboration with Emily Hicks, this project took many forms: conceptual postcards, staged photographs, and a series of site-specific perfomances. Photo by Henry Witkowski.

1988 "THE BIRTH OF BORDER BRUJO"   (in collaboration with Tijuana performance artist Hugo Sánchez) After the two performers crossed the U.S./Mexico border in costume, they performed outside the Centro Cultural de la Raza, Balboa Park, San Diego. Photo by Isaac Artenstein.

1989 "BORDER BRUJO" One of the many hybrid personae of Border Brujo. This photo was taken during the *Border Brujo* film shooting. Photo by Becky Cohen.

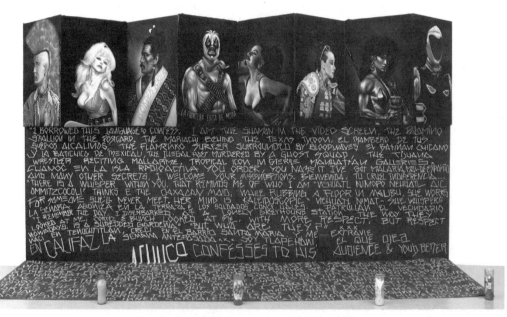

1989 "THE VELVET HALL OF FAME" (8 velvet paintings, graffiti, and candles) Installation by Gómez-Peña at New Langton Arts, San Francisco. This piece was originally created for the Border Arts Workshop project "Border Axis" at Artspace, New York. The velvet paintings are depictions of various Gómez-Peña performance characters in the traditional velvet tourist art style. Painted by Chicana artist Eva García (RIP). The text on the wall is an excerpt from a performance poem titled "Ocnoceni." (Photo by Sixth Street Studio).

1990 "FAMILY PORTRAIT" Coco Fusco as the authentic Cuban rumbera, Gómez-Peña as El Charromántico, and Martha Peña de Gómez as the Cool Suegrao.This is one of a series of performance-photos involving relatives (in this case, Gómez-Peña's mother) staged at an old-fashioned photo studio in Mexico.

1990 "AUTHENTIC CUBAN SANTERA AND EL AZTEC HIGH-TECH WELCOME COLUMBUS WITH RITUAL OFFERINGS" The collaborations of Gómez-Peña and Coco Fusco explore notions of "authenticity" and the artificial construction of ethnic identity by the mainstream. From the project "Norte/Sur," Mexican Museum, San Francisco. Photo by Cristina Taccone.

1992 "TWO UNDISCOVERED AMERINDIANS VISIT SPAIN."
Coco Fusco and Gómez-Peña lived for three days in a golden cage placed at Columbus Plaza in Madrid as "Amerindians from the (fictional) island of Guatinaui." They were taken to the bathroom on leashes and hand-fed through the bars. Audience members could ask for an "authentic dance," a "story in Guatinaui," or a Polaroid. This piece was also performed at Covent Gardens, London; the Walker Art Center, Minneapolis; the Smithsonian Institution, Washington, D.C.; the Museum of Natural History, Sydney, Australia; the Field Museum, Chicago; the Whitney Museum of American Art, New York; and at other locations. Photo by Nancy Lytle.

1991 PERFORMANCE JAMMING SESSION The Space, Boston. These collaborations included artists Gregorio Rivera, Angelica Rivera, Debbie Sanchez-Reed, and Bart Uchida. Photo by Charles Mayer.

1992 "EL WARRIOR FOR GRINGOSTROIKA" Character from a multimedia performance series for *The Year of the White Bear*. Photo courtesy Walker Art Center, Minneapolis.

SIN/TRANSLATION

V. R.º de la R. M. Maria Anna Agueda
Igna.ª prim.ª Priora y fundad.ª d.
Conu.º de Monjas Recoletas de S.
Rosa d. S.ta Maria de la Ciudad
Puebla de l.s Angeles murio
enbr.º d. 1756 año
...

Ortuño.   fec.

SIN / TRANSLATION

(FROM SPANISH TO ENGLISH AND VICE VERSA)

Some of the poetical texts in this section were either broadcast on the radio, performed for video, or performed live as part of a larger project. Others are memories of sorts, letters, descriptions of projects, visual poems, or conceptual postcards. Only a handful of these pieces were ever published before in a strictly literary context.

NOTE: I encourage my monolingual gringo readers to attempt to read the texts in Spanish and Spanglish. I'm sure you will understand them.

My First Performance Ever
(Morelia, 1974)

I enter a church.
I hide behind the pulpit.
3 days pass by.
no one discovers me.
I get bored.
I return to the hotel.
I try to commit suicide.
I receive no phone calls.
I get bored.
I go out to the plaza.
I buy 10 avocados.
I throw them to the cops.
they don't seem to mind.
I get bored.
[The journalists ignore
the importance of my actions.]

EL CRUCE
(SAN YSIDRO, CALIFORNIA, 1978)

cruzo la línea
oscilo
de un lado al otro
de mi esqueleto

now

aguardo sigiloso
puñal en mano
en el estuario de 3 culturas

anti-paisano
I am here to conflict with your plans

LA PARTIDA
(MEXICO, D.F., 1978)

. . . partir es un algo irreversible
hacia el noroeste
la muerte
o el futuro
[pausa]
pero a pesar de todo
termina uno
despidiéndose
largándose
diciendo bye al sol
al charco
a la novia
al vecindario
y con los brazos abiertos
y el corazón de fuera
es uno blanco fácil
de franco-tiradores extranjeros

MINICORRIDO
(LOS ANGELES, 1978)

nací en Tenochtitlán
crecí en el barrio de Santa María
y me extravié en Califas
la semana antepasada
traigo un penny
un mapa arrugado del Paraíso
y unas ganas enormes de joder

INVENTORY OF THE FIRST FOUR MONTHS
OF MY JOURNEY (LOS ANGELES, 1979)

4 months
2 lovers, one in particular
38 days of categoric loneliness
1 crestfallen birthday
28 drawings
50 poetic actions
5 new friends
1 skinny but charming dog
238 tears
13 innovative ideas
2014 peals of laughter
7 mountains
10 freeways
    subtotal: one more immigrant
    total: one less Mexican

NOT TO BE TRANSLATED

QUESTION
(1980)

[to be attached to bathroom mirrors]

The Tribe of the Fiery Pupils inquires:
The European "democracies" are besieged
by terrorism,
Latin America is besieged by para-military
 violence,
the United States is besieged by its own
citizenry.
Which would you prefer—
a terrorist, a soldier, or a psychopath?

RITUAL EVENT
(LOS ANGELES, 1980)

he goes with his immigrant friends to a
nightclub
& dances for a vision:
"they brought me to Paradise
by accident
they left me here
right in the center of the wound"
the bouncer throws him out of the page

ORACIÓN DEL INDIO ENJUALADO
(LOS ANGELES, 1980)

cansado estoy
y cansado permanezco
por los siglos de los siglos
let me loose
cansado estoy
y cansado permanezco
por los siglos de los siglos
let me loose
(ad infinitum)

AMERICA POST-COLOMBINA

1492-1992

PSA
(TRAIN PARIS/BARCELONA, 1980)

I see no rest for your soul
in the coming decade
no place for your body
no structure for your ideas
in the world as it is
it's going to be like
traveling in a noisy train
for 10 years
& not having your ticket
& the porter harassing you
every half hour
& the other passengers
sleeping or drinking
themselves to sleep
believe me
I see no rest for your soul
in the coming decade

MY GENERATION
(LOS ANGELES, 1981)

[excerpt from a Poyesis Genética program]

"My generation generates chaos
witnesses chaos
multiplies chaos . . .
My generation generates incomplete wisdom
produces broken art/fragmented poetry,
anachronistic children . . .
My generation is unable to finish the
    performance.
My generation is unable to complete structures.
Our structures are open-ended out of laziness,
fiaca, hueva, confusión, anger, angustia,
Not out of rigor. It's pitiful.
We lack the necessary rigor to be able
to perpetrate our disjointed traditions of
    rebellion,
to fight the ominous dogma realité . . ."

I Don't Know Where Art Will Take Us
(Los Angeles, 1981)

I don't know where art will take us
I'll probably know on Monday
my shaman is coming over for lunch
he certainly has the answer
maybe 2 or 3
for I am tired of searching myself
I feel the goose bumps of uncertainty
the gases of nihilism in my stomach
I no longer offer resistance to my destiny
I have better things to do
like forgetting or returning
I don't care where art will take us
I go anywhere
[pause]
however, I'll ask my shaman for you
so you can sleep better
I am tired of sleeping myself

for my nightmares are becoming repetitious
however I understand your anxiety
of not knowing whether it's worth the effort
of painting or writing 8 hours a day in the '80s
if the end result is going to be Madness type C
the one that drives you to cut your ear off
play the bonzo at the UN Plaza
or hang yourself from the Eiffel Tower
in the name of performance art
[pause]
I'd rather travel
I want to see enough ugliness & shit
before I make the Big Commitment
before I cut my wrists with a poem
or hang myself in an installation piece
compadre believe me
I just don't know where art will take us.

Punk Angst
(Zurich, 1982)

sometimes I feel
I should shave my head
tattoo my face with Chinese calligraphy
buy me a leather jumpsuit
(made out of elephant scrotum)
& fly back to Mexico
to scare my relatives & friends
sometimes I feel ex-cátedra
(I mean the sky is full of rockets
& the earth is filled with everybody's caca)
The question is
should I perform tomorrow or not?

PERFORMANCE PHONE CALL
(LUCERNE, 1982)

On a certain day in Lucerne, I entered a 5-star
hotel and told the person at the front desk that I
was in room 69 and I needed to make a long-
distance call. She believed me. She even handed
me a martini. My mother answered in tears:
"mama, I love you
I just performed my best piece ever
in a 5-star hotel . . .
[interference]
no, there are no pirates in Lake Lucerne
¿que?
40% of Mexico City is unemployed?
the peso is down to 150?
[interference]
listen, tell papa it's just a dream
& that I am still 5 years old
no, I am not in Europe
it's only a bad dream . . .
[interference]
tell him to look for me in the garden
if he doesn't find me there
maybe the dream is still not clear enough . . .
[interference]
yes, the Europeans are treating me fine . . .
no, this is not true
they are kind of . . . selfish
well, this is not completely true either
my friends are alright
but they are ex-Europeans
nevermind, I am tired . . .

tell me, is it true that Mexico
right now is closer to hell than the U.S.?
[pause]
you are kidding me . . .
yes, I'm doing fine
I don't have time to get sick or depressed
even if I do
I miss the sun, the huapango, your enchiladas
but I don't regret this journey
I'm practically the only Mexican here
I feel like Chicano Alice in Wonderland
but directed by Bertolucci or Albicoco
I row every night under the fog
therefore I think of you quite often
I thank you both
for everything you ever did for me
[interference]
I heard that Adriana married a businessman
tell her that in revenge
I'll marry a travel agent
sorry mama
I know this is irrelevant
but my heart is broken . . .
[interference]
. . . I mean broken . . .
[interference]
mama I love you
look for me in the garden or the mirror . . ."
[The line gets disconnected.]

EL ARTISTA FRONTERIZO
(TIJUANA-SAN DIEGO, 1983)

[*Poema/manifesto*]
el poeta ilegal
el pintor indocumentado
el mexicano que regresa o se va
el que se fúe en la placenta de su madre
o en la cajuela de un Buick
el enjaulado/amortajado
el máscara de escroto y terciopelo
el bilingüe lingüe
el bicéfalo/bifálico
el que speaks Spanglish sabroso
el que spikin-inglish o te chingo
el que I don't know what you mean
el que róe su cordón umbilical
el que sangra y extraña
el que perdió su sentido de orientación
el que asesinaron cuando soñaba
inmerso en su radio de transistores
el que arroja sueños-molotov al otro lado

el que anda de visita sin visa
el que viene de paso y no pasa
el que medio pasa y se atora
el que núnca regresa
o regresa a medias
ya sin piernas
sin lengua ni memoria
ese soy yo
eso somos nosotros
los vatos intersticiales
y eso precisely serán ustedes
actores de una épica fantasma
que apenas se distingue
en el mapa de la gran conciencia
y ningún proyecto
de amor, arte o protesta
será completado
si no se realiza en ambas orillas y lenguas

POSTCARD
(NUEVA YORK, 1983)

Madre:
un día regresaré
cargado de dólares imaginarios
invertiré mi fortuna
en algo inservible pero bello
un banco de metáforas tal vez
un club de sexo oral
o una academia de danza marina
quizá me alcance para todo
y hasta me sobre
para mi propio entierro

DIDACTIC PHONE CALL
(SAN DIEGO, 1984)

[*With thick Mexican accent*]
"sorry caballero, but . . .
Castillian Spanish is not better than 'Mexican'
it's not even spoken anymore
no, nachos aren't indigenous food
they are not even food . . .
no, buñuelo is a dessert not a filmmaker
you mean Buñuel . . .
no, he wasn't Mexican . . .
no, Lorca was also a Spaniard
believe me
Tijuana is not that dangerous
there is no typhoid down there . . .
it's all in your mind
the Aztecs weren't cannibals
& the PRI is not the only political party
there are many others
but that's beside the point
the real issue is not my country, caballero
I'm afraid it is your IQ . . ."
Next day I receive a death threat.

EL 7 MÁSCARAS [SUPER-HÉROE FRONTERIZO]
(TIJUANA, 1984)

[*Soundtrack: "Mambo del Auletero" by Pérez Prado*]

yo soy
el 7 máscaras
que si, que no
el 7 máscaras
que soy, que fuí
que siempre seré

yo soy el brother Tlatoani
que si, que no
el brother Tlatoani
regreso cabisbajo del la pisca
estaciono mi buick
& me arrojo a los brazos
de mi prieta

yo soy el ruletero
que si, que no
el taxi driver
llevo turistas
a los linderos del Mictlán
& de paso los despojo
de su ignorancia

yo soy el Rayo Dislocado
que si, que no
el Rayo Dislocado
pirómano y agitador de ficheras
me buscan por amar & no pagar
por aquello de ser libre
de palabra & pito

yo soy el Icui-ricui
que si, que no
el Icaro-cundicui
brujo incógnito conecta-yerbabuena
traigo alas nuevas
zapato tenis
& nada me detiene

yo soy el Radio-Activo
que si, que no
el Radio-Activo
disc-jockey del 3er Apocalípsis
me deslizo & a todos radioalcanzo
& en dólares me pagan pues

yo soy el Diplo-matic
que si, que no
el Diplo-matic
voy voy de país en país
unificando al personal
& tramando guerrillas conceptuales

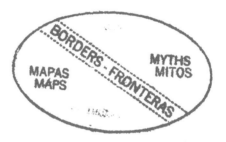

yo soy el vato relamido
que si, que no
el va todo lamido
soy nada & en la nada me revuelco
me encuentran & no me buscan
& en la movida
me explayo & multiplico

yo soy quien soy
post-punk el 7 máscaras
& vivo a 1/2 cuadra
del fín
de la cultura occidental.

UNTRANSLATABLE BORDER PRAYER
(INNER SITE, 1984)

"Tata Dios el que embotella
Patrocinador del Gran Desmadre
Descuartizador de espejos & alcancías
Justiciero de tele-ilusiones
tú
que con tanta soltura te retratas
a la salida de una nube
& que tan agusto flotas
cuál papalote en la estratósfera
tú
que con tanto esmero imprimes
estampitas psicotrópicas
en nuestras frentes
tú que todo
tú que nada
dános la suficiente cohesión molecular
para regresar intactos
y manten nuestros sueños
suspendidos
en hilos de nylon
aunque sea por una noche
no te hagas del rogar
no te hagas el mister etéreo."

TWO FRAGMENTS OF "TIJUANA/NIRVANA"
(1985)

[*These fragments appeared on the bilingual radio project "Border-X-Frontera,"
created in collaboration with playwright David Schein.*]

I

EL REFERI BINACIONAL

[*Voice of a Mexican wrestling referee. Soundtrack:
bullfight music*]
"en esta noche de gala
palenke del Nuevo Mundo
habrán de enfrentarse a muerte
los monstruos de la historia
& el lenguaje
con ustedes
el Robin Hood Ramírez
con su puñado de naked mariachis
expertos en border-x-tensiones
en esta esquina
el Santo
sultán de Contadora
en aquella
Supermán number two
guarura del Pentágono
en esta otra
la Momia Tarahumara
alias Rarámuri en patínes
& en aquesta
Sor Godzilla
Vuestra Ñora Protectora
de la Línea

levanten apuestas & plegarias
derramen saliva & esperma
en cuadrilíteros binacionales
recontragriten
que la vida es una & loca
como dice Fact Pachuco
dice el vato filosso,
the North is in our minds
sssuaveee!
the South is in your pocket
eeeeessee!
the East is on your left hand
buzzzooo!
and the West is now!
watchaaa!
la extrema derecha del paraísso
so buzo caperuzo con los rusos
que como dice el navy aquel
let's barricade utopia
de púas balazos & ladridos
que de púas y balazos
es la mismísima palabra del señor"
Oh Lord, pas qué mal pedoi

157

II
EL MEDICINE MEROLICO

[*Voice of a street vendor. Soundtrack: sounds of Revolución Avenue on a Saturday night*]

¿qué le damos caballero?
¿qué le toco señorita?
¿qué le duele?
¿qué la falla?
no se atore
passee usted
we know what's on your mind
a dollar a joint
a poisoned taco
an authentic Aztec watch
a scrotum T-shirt
the secret of Huitchilopochtli
the tits of La Tigresa
10 extras for your new film
let's pact Doctor Calak
we know what's on your pocket
lo que es today
tomorrow no es
lo que pulsa & hierve
al ratito se coagula
o mejor dicho PO-E-TA
& valga la cacofonía
flor que orinas no amanece
taxi que pasa no vuelve
artista que sufre no vende
bacha que lames no prende
por lo tanto señorita
no se agüite sueñe ahorita
que la revolución comienza aquí
en la catre/la botella
la entrepierna
chew me chola
chew me sabrosso
hasta el fondo & el cansancio
tritúrame
hasta la última molécula
vampirízame
draculébrame
¡uuhhhhaaaagggggaaayy!
que al fin mañana resucito"

VAMPIRO REPUBLICANO

ORACIÓN AL SANTO PATRÓN
DE LOS DESCOLGADOS
(TIJUANA, 1985)

[*A prayer to be told before going on tour*]
Santo Patrón de los Descolgados
afila nuestros colmillos
y resérvanos 3 literas
que mañana nos vamos de gira
desde Mérida hasta Houston
y luego hacia Nueva York
a llevar el mensaje de La Raza:
"El hombre chicano se desprende
de su caparazón"

BICONCEPTION
(TIJUANA/SAN DIEGO, 1985)

[*Pre-project of erotic-artistic-political activism*]

A. A Mexican man (preferably a cholo) and a North American woman (preferably a punk) meet at midnight at the border fence, each on his/her respective side. She is in her most fertile state. They undress, and proceed to fondle each other through the barbed wire with their fingertips. With extreme care and a clear historical consciousness, they begin the binational coitus. She gets pregnant despite the border.

B. The baby is born nine months later at the intersection of Playas de Tijuana and Border Field State Park (the end of the border and the beginning of the Pacific Ocean/the end of Western civilization, and the northernmost point of Latin America). Two doctors, a Mexican and an Anglo-Saxon, assist the birth.

C. The parents demand dual citizenship for the child.

D. The child is educated at the best schools in both countries, and spends time with cultural and political leaders from both Americas. One day, she/he will become the most important leader of the new transcontinental culture.

LA REPÚBLICA FLOTANTE
DE TRANSTERRÁNIA
(SAN DIEGO, 1985)

. . . transterrados caminamos hacia el norte
cruzamos fronteras a empujones
buscamos lo nuestro
lo heredado y expropiado
lo traducido ilegalmente
y somos tantos
que ya formamos
una nación invisible
que nadie ha logrado bautizar

. . . en tierra extraña vivimos
sin tregua ni filiación
desdibujamos mapas
rebautizamos volcanes
étnias, meridianos y satélites
lo re-nombramos todo
en espanglish y esperanto
desnombramos
lo que otros bautizaron
sin autorización de los dioses

CONFESSION TO AN IMAGINARY PRIEST
(BARCELONA HOSPITAL, 1986)

performance was always my salvation
what I didn't do as a citizen
I did in the name of art
& no one seemed to mind

I broke a zillion laws
in the realms of
politics, identity & language
& everytime I broke a rule
I had a conversation with Death
in each of these conversations
she told me to be more careful the next time

Tonight I proceed with absolute caution

IDENTIDAD EN CRISIS
IDENTIDAD EN CRISIS

SOUND LETTER #2
[Transcript of a recording]

Today, September 12, 1986, exactly one month before the "discovery of America," I visited the Plaza Colón. At the Centro Cultural Villa de Madrid, there is a waterfall-shaped fountain facing a map which portrays Columbus' first trip from Palos (August 3, 1492) to San Salvador Island (October 12, 1492).

I took a sip of water from the fountain and turned on my tape recorder. I stepped on the map area and asked an Israeli tourist to take a photo of myself mimicking Columbus' heroic statue.

I said in Spanish: "I have come back to Spain in the name of the migrant Tribe of the Fiery Pupils. I have come back to reclaim the continent of America, to un-discover it, so to speak. I speak for the millions of artists and thinkers from the other continent who wish to erase Columbus' legacy from mankind's tortured memory. It's me, Telpócatl, el Siete Máscaras and . . ."

A crowd began to gather around me. The Israeli tourist freaked out and ran away. Two members of the Spanish Guardia Civil were observing the event with distrust. "I am a performance tourist," I explained to them before they approached me, "I'm just recording a sound letter for my compadres in the New World." They cracked up and left.

Since the tourist ran away, I have no photographs of this performance.

Signed:

Gómez-Peña,
alias Cristóbal Cogelón,
"El Indocumentado"

EL VAMPIRO INVERTIDO
(MEXICO CITY, 1986)

on one of my trips back to Mexico
I brought this Gila monster in a bag
as a present to my neighbour
"El Vampiro Invertido"
—he looked like one—
he trained the Gila monster
& developed a performance skit for the zócalo:
The monster would count to 12 with his tail
while "El Vampiro" recited his very awful
    poetry
stuff like,

"Tesmogtitlán
D.F.ctuoso
Detrítus Defecalis
Mexicou Cida
Ecocidio sin par
parranda apocalíptic
ciudad de mi apestosa
y recontrapoluted juventusss
a ver si devienes ancianita
a ver si llegas al nuevo siglo
exiliada en tu pirámide de azufre
ad infinitum . . ."

& so on & so forth
until the cops arrived
& his epic ended for good

HUMBLE GOALS
(1987)

. . . but before the coffin opens
one has some basic duties
for example
to go back to Madrid
one Sunday morning
at the Puerta del Sol
declare the 2nd Mexican Independence
& then go to Vatican City
& proclaim the separation
of the Latin American church
once & for all
go to Paris in a rainy day
& declare the autonomy
of our writers & winters
& from there to Washington
on Christmas
announce default with a sax
& ban all nuclear weapons
[pause]
& only then
can one go back
to the old neighborhood
kick a couple of dogs
knock at her door
give her a kiss good-bye
& begin to walk into the night
to wait for the coffin to pick you up
[At this point
my audience begins to wonder
why Mexicans are so obsessed with Death.]

PREPARATION FOR
RITUAL BORDER CROSSING
(DAY OF THE DEAD, TIJUANA, 1987)

I cut my hair
at the Peluquería Rex
as an offering to Discoatlicue
diosa de la tierra loca
I prepare myself
for the grand border crossing
through the window
I see a skeleton heading North
"vato"—he says
"no claudiques
escupe tu pinche mantra
y recupera el terreno perdido
. . . pero de ya!"

EL CIEGUITO/THE BLIND MAN
(1987)

[This piece was written during a binational pilgrimage from the Tijuana
Municipal cemetery to the Centro Cultural de la Raza in San Diego. Twelve
artists from both sides participated in this event. I crossed the border as a 'blind
man' with opaque glasses and a cane. The border guard didn't ask for my papers;
he felt compassion, I guess. I was speaking to a cassette recorder.]

. . . te veo
monjita pintarrajeada
te veo y no te creo
el sci-fi rocker
te traigo finto
marine sangrante
yo te abomino
bajo la niebla
te fiscalizo
sultán de 1,000 encuentros
pinto mi cruz
la wrestling diva
Pantera del Norte
te veo y te deseo
borrachita del Chicago
te veo, te meo

pankraca maraquera
antiér contagíaste la peste
Madona de la Crisis Binacional
te veo y te sigo deseando
le chola punk de la frontiere
te veo
me matas
me arrepiento
me parto en dos, en diéz
me desintegro
negrura total
[en el centro del escenario
el águila bate sus últimas plumas
y la migra me dispara por la espalda
oh Lord, pus que mal pedo]

LOS DESCOYUNTADOS
(MÉRIDA, 1987)

nacimos en el cemento
mamamos leche y Pepsi Cola
crecimos descoyuntados
entre Mérida y New York
franqueados por cables y cocoteros
admiramos a los mayas y a los Stones
seducimos gringas descalzas
sobre lajas precortesianas
tramamos revoluciones
en estudios de grabación
practicamos tantra y cine
coleccionamos trizas de mil tradiciones
las reordenamos al aventón
y de tanto viajar de sur a norte
del pasado al futuro
y viceversa
perdimos la mentada nocion del tiempo

DISLOCATED
[TRANSLATION]

we were born on the pavement
we were nursed on milk and Pepsi
we grew up dislocated
between Mérida and New York
linked by cables and coconut palm trees
we admired the Mayans and the Rolling Stones
we seduced barefoot gringas
on pre-Cortesian stone slabs
we plotted revolutions
in recording studios
we practiced tantra and film
we gathered fragments from a thousand traditions
we rearranged them at will
and from so much traveling
from North to South
from past to future
and vice versa
we lost the much-touted sense of time

PUNCTURED TIRE
(HIGHWAY 5, CALIFORNIA, 1988)

I am stuck in the middle of the journey
a highway without human activity
a text without visible structure
life on this side of the border
on your side . . .
I no longer know who I am
but I like it

REWRITING LIFE ON STAGE
(SEATTLE, 1988)

. . . & the Mexican children I didn't have
will have to confront me one day
Papá
if only the country
had been in better shape
when you decided to part
if only you had done
something more tangible
with your life
like staying
& becoming a poet in Spanish
but instead partíste
cruzaste la frontera del etcétera
y te extraviáste en la tierra del control
& now
10 years later
you rewrite your life on stage
dragging before you
all these innocent souls

are you fully responsible for your actions
or is this just an open rehearsal?

LETTER
(TIJUANA, 1990)

Dear Self #2:
I feel a bit lonely tonight
Ruben returned to El Salvador
Coco went back to Havana
Marco left for New York
Amalia is in Spain
Alfredo is in jail
& I am back in Tijuana
others like Elia, Isaac & Max
are nowhere to be found

are we migrating in reverse?
or are we simply collecting data for
    future projects?

PERFORMANCE FUNERAL
(SAN FRANCISCO, 1990)

I'm currently organizing my own funeral
the press release states:
"authentic Latino performance artist
indocumentado #00281419
dies on stage from consciousness attack
the critics chant in chorus
'we finally got it!
we finally got it!'
he leaves a one-year-old chicanito
5 books in progress
25 unedited videos
& 96 unpublished scripts
all passionately staged
in the most unlikely places
like convents, cantinas & detention centers
the community is invited to attend the ceremony
at the Museum of Lost Identity
dirección conocida U.S.A.
there will be lots of colorful surprises
a norteño group on the left wing
a punk band on the right wing
& a 10-meter-tall multimedia altar on the
    Main Hall
despite his will
Coors will donate the beer
& El Torito, the barbecue burritos
don't hesitate to attend
even if only as a corpse
we expect something real crazy from the guy
as we all know,
Latinos are unpredictable by nature"
                                signed: BORDER BRUJO

THE TEN COMMANDMENTS
OF BELSE-BUSH
(LOS ANGELES, 1990)

[*This text was later performed as a PSA for a project
with the Experimental Sound Studio of Chicago. It
was delivered in the voice of a fundamentalist
preacher.*]
thou shalt not evade taxes
thou shalt not be poor or ill
thou shalt not get pregnant
thou shalt not buy a home
thou shalt not talk back to cops
thou shalt not disagree with foreign policy
thou shalt not be a foreigner or speak a foreign
    language
thou shalt not make controversial art
thou shalt not demand an explanation
thous shalt not demand access to the media
[repeat in loop]

The Broken Line
[La Línea Quebrada

THERE
used to be
A

Mexican

PERFORMANCE

ARTIST

ON THIS PAGE,

BUT...

Dear fellow citizen of the end-of-the-century society:

We approach the last decade of the twentieth century submerged in total perplexity as we witness, from the U.S./Mexico border region, structural changes in the world topography.

We can't help but feel like uninvited actors in a disnarrative science-fiction film with the following plot:

THE COLD WAR ENDS AS THE U.S. DRUG WAR BEGINS. THE SOUTH REPLACES THE EAST AS THE NEW THREATENING OTHERNESS. RUSSIA IMPLEMENTS PERESTROIKA AND GLASNOST. A NEW ERA OF EAST/WEST RELATIONS BEGINS. THE CHINESE STATE CARRIES OUT THE MASSACRE OF TIANANMEN SQUARE. THE BERLIN WALL IS ABOLISHED EXACTLY WHEN THE UNITED STATES BEGINS TO MILI-TARIZE ITS BORDER WITH MEXICO. HUNGARY, POLAND, BULGARIA, AND CZECHOSLOVAKIA EXPERIENCE AN INSTANTANEOUS, RELA-TIVELY PACIFIC TRANSITION TOWARD "DEMOCRACY." THE SALVADOREAN CIVIL WAR REACHES A STALEMATE. ROMANIAN DICTATOR NICOLAE CEAUSESCU FALLS WHILE CHILEAN DICTATOR PINOCHET LOSES THE AWAITED FIRST DEMOCRATIC ELECTION SINCE THE FALL OF PRESIDENT ALLENDE. CENTRAL AMERICA AND MEXICO MOVE TO THE RIGHT. AND TO THE OUTRAGE OF THE INTER-NATIONAL COMMUNITY, THE UNITED STATES INVADES PANAMA.

The birth pains of the new millennium are overwhelming. We don't know what will happen next. The amount, complexity, and intensity of the changes surpass our capability to digest them and codify them adequately.

For the moment, as much as we can aspire to is recognizing collectively that (1) drastically different relationships between East and West and therefore between North and South are being developed; (2) the centers of power are irreversibly shifting; (3) a new international society is being born, and (4) a new culture will have to emerge from its foundation.

In the United States there is a movement toward tolerance and reform that is equivalent to glasnost and that is mistakenly called multiculturalism; there are aggressive government sectors devoted to its destruction.

As border artists, we wonder what our role will be in this whole process. Should we be chroniclers, activists, philosophers, or diplomats? And what kind of art must we make to contribute to a world dialogue?

For the moment, as Europe prepares for the grand opening of its borders, we are preparing ourselves for another major project: the grand redefinition of 1992. We won't be celebrating the "discovery of America" or the "encounter of cultures." We will be attending a funeral for all the victims of five hundred years of genocide of our indigenous cultures.

This text and the accompanying image (map of the world with a bone cross) were created by Guillermo Gómez-Peña and Robert Sanchez. In different forms (mural or installation), it has been presented at the Meeting of the Worlds Festival in Finland, recreated in Barcelona under the title Five Hundred Years of Genocide at the invitation of the Joan Miró Foundation, and published in various magazines as a performance. The two columns of text are meant either to be read by two persons speaking at the same time or to be broadcast on separate tracks simultaneously.
(Warning: by the time this piece is exhibited, published, or broadcast in your country, the informa-

EL MEXICAN'T
(CHICAGO, 1992)

[*Soundtrack: Agustín Lara*]
I sometimes wake up in the middle of the night
with a hole in my chest
lava running down my eyes
the sheets all covered with blood
my inner radio playing a scratchy bolero
I wake up alone
within the sinister emptiness of America
[Red spotlight on me]
I begin to cry like a baby coyote
I long for the garden of my childhood
& the blatant affection of my relatives &
	neighbors
who always forgave my excesses and
	contradictions
[Music stops.]
I stand up & go to the bathroom sink
[close-up]
I look at my face in the mirror

. . . 14 years older since I left
"I used to be a Mexican" I whisper
"I used to be a Mexican"
"I used to speak Spanish"
I put on one of my performance masks
la del Warrior for Gringostroika
then I go back to sleep
I dream of my father who died in Tenochtitlán
right as my son was being born in California
I wake up 4 years later
in a country at war
in a city at war
my audience is all composed
by victims of political torture
they don't know it
they don't remember
they don't want to remember
[The audience begins to cry.]

BORDER AIDS/PANIC POLITICS

GUILLERMO GÓMEZ-PEÑA

Writer and experimental artist Guillermo Gómez-Peña was born in Mexico City and came to the United States in 1978. Since that time, he has been exploring border issues, cross-cultural identity, and U.S./Latino cultural relations with the use of multiple media: journalism, performance, radio art, video, bilingual poetry, and installation art. From 1984 to 1990, he was a founding member of the Border Arts Workshop/Taller de Arte Fronterizo. From 1987 to 1990, he was a contributor to the national radio program "Crossroads." He is currently a contributing editor to *High Performance* magazine and the *Drama Review*. He has received the Prix de la Parole at the International Theatre Festival of the Americas (1989), the New York Bessie Award (1989), and a MacArthur Foundation Fellowship (1991).

This book was designed by Jean Foos and Dirk Rowntree. It is set in ITC Galliard type by The Typeworks, and manufactured by Friesen Printers on acid-free paper.

Additional Photo Credits. Front cover: detail from the photo on page 134. Back cover: photo courtesy of SPARC. Dedication page: detail from "El Warrior for Gringostroika," photo courtesy Walker Art Center, see page 139. Page 35: detail from "El Moctezuma, Jr." Photo courtesy Walker Art Center. Page 65: detail of photo by Biff Henrich. Page 79: "Border Brujo," photo by Max Aguilera-Hellweg.